Children, Parenthood, and Social
Welfare in the Context of
Developmental Psychology

Children, Parenthood, and Social Welfare in the Context of Developmental Psychology

MICHAEL SIEGAL
Senior Lecturer in Psychology, University of Queensland

CLARENDON PRESS · OXFORD
1985

Oxford University Press, Walton Street, Oxford OX2 6DP

Oxford   New York   Toronto
Delhi   Bombay   Calcutta   Madras   Karachi
Kuala Lumpur   Singapore   Hong Kong   Tokyo
Nairobi   Dar es Salaam   Cape Town
Melbourne   Auckland

and associated companies in
Beirut   Berlin   Ibadan   Nicosia

Oxford is a trade mark of Oxford University Press

Published in the United States
by Oxford University Press, New York

British Library Cataloguing in Publication Data

Siegal, Michael
Children, parenthood, and social welfare in
the context of developmental psychology.
1. Cognition in children   2. Social psychology
I. Title
155.4'13   BF723.C5
ISBN 0-19-852120-0

Library of Congress Cataloging in Publication Data
Siegal, Michael
Children, parenthood, and social welfare in
the context of developmental psychology.
Bibliography: p.
Includes indexes.
1. Child development.   2. Developmental psychology.
3. Parenthood.   4. Family policy.   I. Title.
HQ772.S494   1985   305.2'3   85-6696
ISBN 0-19-852120-0

Set by Eta Services (Typesetters) Ltd., Beccles, Suffolk
Printed in Great Britain
at the University Press, Oxford
by David Stanford
Printer to the University

Preface

Thunder and lightning occur together. Thunder comes after lightning. But that does not mean that lightning causes thunder.

Explanations in terms of antecedent relationships or regularity of occurrence are not sufficient to establish a causal link between variables. Causal explanations are particularly difficult to come by in the social sciences, especially in developmental psychology which concerns the study of changes in children's behaviour over time.

This book picks up where an earlier one left off (Siegal 1982). It reviews data which are often based on correlational studies of child development. Since these are limited to demonstrations of regularity of occurrence, strong causal inferences are premature and unjustified. But together with the growing body of evidence based on the experimental manipulation of variables, correlational studies provide directions for further research which hold out the possibility of establishing causal connections.

Drawing upon studies of both adults and children, development is examined in a context involving parents, peers, and society. The socioeconomic conditions of the family are seen to transform parenthood and parent–child interaction through processes of social cognition, identification, and internalization. These processes can have a role in determining the influences which parents and children have on each other and which affect the child outside the family. In turn, children's perceptions of their social world are viewed to affect their moral development and intellectual performance. The overall aim of the book is to integrate theories of development toward a more complete understanding of the nature of the connections between child development and social welfare.

My work has proceeded with the fine cooperation of children from preschool (3–4 years), kindergarten (5 years), and grade 1 (6 years) through to grade 12 (17–18 years), and I acknowledge the many parents and teachers who provided assistance. I am grateful to the Australian Research Grants Scheme and the University Research Grants Committee of the University of Queensland for their support. I appreciate the hospitality of the Department of Experimental

Psychology, Oxford University, where a first draft of the book was written while I was on a sabbatical leave.

I am indebted to my colleagues and students. Those who merit special mention are John Bain, Mary Barclay, Robin Francis, Kym Irving, Robyn Nugent, Jenny Sanderson, David Shwalb, Rebecca Storey, Phyllis Tharenou, and Lorraine Waters. Behind each of these pages is the contribution of my wife Sharon.

A version of Chapter 1 appeared in the *Journal of Applied Developmental Psychology* (1984, **5**, 124–44), and a version of Chapter 7 was published in *Imagination, Cognition and Personality* (1984, **3**, 337–51). The tables in Chapter 4 are reproduced by permission of the Society for Research in Child Development, Inc., and the figures in Chapter 6 by permission of North Holland Publishing Company.

Brisbane   M.S.
January 1985

Contents

1 Socioeconomic conditions and the quality of parent–child relations: a trickle-down view   1

2 Moral development in context   18

3 Intellectual performance in context   45

4 Parents, peers, and children's appraisals of others' behaviour   59

5 Morality and criminal justice: a first group of effects   83

6 Achievement and economic justice: a second group of effects   97

7 Agreement, conflict, and control   112

8 Development as reflected by changes in the nature of parenthood: a bubble-up view   125

References   139

Author index   163

Subject index   169

I

Socioeconomic conditions and the quality of parent–child relations: a trickle-down view

Children's perceptions of the self and others contribute to the quality of parent–child relations. Yet the importance of perceptions has often been perfunctorily acknowledged and then neglected in accounts of child development. Some of these deal with parents' self-reported or observed behaviour toward children. Alternatively, we have parent–child relations described as a product or byproduct of children's general cognitive development.

To dwell exclusively on parental behaviour and general cognitive processes without examining perceptions of the self and others is somewhat like attempting to record a child's height without bothering to anchor the tape measure on the floor. To right this balance, a picture is presented here which directly connects children's perceptions to their behaviour. It involves an examination of the effects of a parenthood which is controlled to a considerable extent by political and economic decisions.

While not suppressing the importance of other factors, the perceptions which children have of their parents (or caretakers) are of special theoretical significance. Comparisons derived from the 'symbolic interactionist' school of social psychology have been made of the importance to children of their perceptions of parental attitudes and behaviour with the actual characteristics observed by researchers or reported by the parents themselves (Acock and Bengston 1980; Davies and Kandel 1981; Scheck and Emerick 1976). These studies suggest that children's perceptions are more predictive of their own attitudes and behaviours than are reports or observations of actual parental characteristics, to the extent that the two types of measures diverge. Perceptions mediate children's behaviour and are partly built upon parental characteristics as immersed within particular socioeconomic contexts and circumstances.

To understand the implications for issues in developmental psychology, we must consider context. It leads us first to an exploration of the trickle-down model of economic activity and the effects of family environment variables.

Parents and children: a trickle-down view

Recently, there has been much debate over the extent to which the industrial West has experienced an economic recession. But regardless of the extent to which it can be said that the effects of a recession have been felt, and the prospects for the future, there is no doubt that economic difficulties currently worry many families. In this vein, a great amount of concern has been voiced in the press and other media over the relationship between economic difficulty and the maintenance of family relationships. To take just one of the kaleidoscope of articles on the issue, Ellen Goodman, writing in *The Guardian Weekly* (25 July 1982, p. 16), reports that 'There are real horror stories from the Midwest about the rising rates of child abuse among the unemployed'.

Parallel to this popular concern, a groundswell of theory has grown around the basic idea that the stress of providing for children's needs in a time of shrinking employment opportunities and rising inflation has impaired the security and unity of the family, and that many recent technological advances have been fundamentally incompatible with social welfare (Giarini 1980; Giarini and Louberge 1978). A pessimistic view is that, under these conditions, the working world of parents seems to have little to offer the young and that some children become prone to behaviour problems and delinquency. Moreover, under conditions of economic decline, some parents may come to regard children as more of a burden than a blessing; in extreme cases, dismal economic prospects might lead to child abuse and neglect.

We begin to explore the validity of this proposition in its two aspects by examining the evidence on parent–child relations in a context of undesirable economic change and economic deprivation. The term 'deprivation' has been used in a great many ways (Brown and Madge 1982, pp. 13–42). However, it can be defined to include at least two types of circumstances. For example, it can consist of a sharp decline in a family's previous affluence owing to layoffs and unemployment (a 'type A'). Alternatively, deprivation can consist of poverty relative to affluence expressed in terms of a low percentage figure of family income relative to the average or normal earnings of a community at large. This may be indicated by the income component of social class measures (a deprivation 'type B').

In contrast to economic deprivation, the quality of parent–child relations might not be as easily depicted in quantitative terms. But clearly 'quality' can be defined to exclude, at the very least, children's abuse and neglect of adult rights, life, and property, commonly termed as problem behaviour or delinquency. From the perspective of parents' relationship with children, it can be defined to at least exclude the physical abuse and neglect of children. There are of course other, less tangible relationships between parents and children which can be deemed subquality and which are researchable against a backdrop of economic deprivation. The focus here, however, will be on the quality of parent–child relations in a clearly identifiable, overtly physical sense, particularly as shown by the absence of children's and adolescents' behaviour problems and by the absence of child abuse and neglect.

Relationships between the workplace and the family will be examined with respect to an extension of a trickle-down model of economic activity. Though other rival models exist, the trickle-down model appears to give an apt characterization of much current economic policy in non-Communist countries. According to Cook and Pearlman (1981), the model consists of six stages and can be outlined as follows: (1) the stimulation of business through direct benefits to entrepreneurs creates; (2) increased business income; followed by (3) growth in new investments; investment in turn (4) creates new jobs and (5) increased fulfilment of the absolute economic needs of the poor. Then in stage 6, the needs of the poor are fulfilled relative to those in the community at large, income differentials are narrowed and there is increased equality for all. Conversely, the trickle-down model states that increased economic deprivation is a product of lack of stimulation to business which serves to shrink business income, new investments, resulting in fewer new jobs, and diminished fulfilment of the relative and absolute needs of the poor.

Except for a short time in the 1960s, it can be said that since 1945 the American strategy for reducing economic inequality has been oriented in varying degrees toward the trickle-down model rather than toward a 'bubble-up' approach which would stimulate economic activity by initially directing resources to the needy in order to increase the purchasing power of the poor. Some of the most salient economic policies pursued in Australia and Britain since the late 1970s have also been of the trickle-down variety.

Whether the trickle-down model works or misfires has been a matter of longstanding controversy among economists (see, for example, Bauer 1981; Robinson 1968; Wagar 1970). Economics has long been lampooned as an imprecise science. All the same, regardless of whether or not trickle-down policy reduces or exacerbates economic deprivation, downward directional effects are assumed. Though little is known about the strength and durability of such effects, they have been viewed to transform what Bronfenbrenner (1977) has called the 'exosystem', the network of relations between groups and institutions which encompass the developing child and exert indirect, though powerful, effects on children's development at a particular point in time. Changes in the exosystem give rise to changes in the 'mesosystem' of relationships between family and school settings.

At stage 6 of the trickle-down model, both the exosystem and the mesosystem of the economically deprived have been altered. Work settings are transformed by changing business conditions with accompanying changes in family economic circumstances. These in turn produce changes in interfamilial and interschool relations.

In this context, the trickle-down model at stage 6 can be extended downwards further to examine the extent to which undesirable economic changes in the exosystem and mesosystem eventually enter into the 'microsystem', the complex of direct relations between the child and the immediate home setting (a trickle-down stage 7). In terms of an extended trickle-down framework, the downward effects of economic decisions can be examined in at least two ways; first, by viewing economic deprivation as it affects the parental image conveyed to children, and in turn at perceptions of parents as these mediate children's behaviour; second, by viewing undesirable economic conditions in the exosystem as these trickle down to affect directly parents' psychological wellbeing and childrearing capabilities, particularly as shown by the incidence of child abuse and neglect. The first, then, is an instance of economic deprivation as it affects the quality of children's behaviour toward adults; the second is an instance of deprivation affecting parents' behaviour toward children. In both instances, mention will be made of the interrelations between schooling and the family. Following Bronfenbrenner, such interrelations could be regarded as processes within the mesosystem, those which could moderate trickle-down effects from the exosystem to the microsystem.

Reference will be made to longitudinal studies which reveal evidence on the issue of whether types of economic deprivation in these two cases can be regarded as antecedents or merely as correlates of parent–child relations. Through longitudinal studies which observe the same subjects at different points in time, it is possible to determine whether changing socioeconomic conditions are followed by changes in the quality of parent–child relations. Moreover, economic effects on parent–child relations can be explored as apart from non-economic ones.

Case number 1: Economic deprivation, perceptions of parents, and children's problem behaviour

Children are not usually direct witnesses of plant closings and queues for welfare cheques. Trickle-down policies affect children indirectly by transforming the work settings of parents within the exosystem, influencing the economic circumstances of the family. These effects trickle down further in permeating the microsystem by conveying an image of deprivation to children through the parents. In turn, unfavourable perceptions of parents with regard to their status as occupational role models reduce children's willingness to comply with adult directives and may generalize in the form of a disrespect for the adult working world and the corporate and legal institutions comprised within the exosystem.

At the same time, across a diversity of educational and social class levels, the young believe that they are entitled to good jobs commensurate with their skills (Derber 1978). Perhaps for these reasons, when expectations of success at finding rewarding employment are seen to be unrealizable, children have difficulty in coming to terms with the adult world. As Bronfenbrenner (1979, p. 271) has written, 'It is probably no coincidence that in today's society as work opportunities for school-aged children and youth have reached new low levels, school achievement has been decreasing at the same time that vandalism and juvenile delinquency in the streets have been on the rise'.

Both studies of problem behaviour in families undergoing a period of hardship during depressed economic conditions as well as studies of the relationship between social class and delinquency point to a connection between children's behaviour and perceptions of parents and the working world.

Type A evidence

Type A evidence has come from the vast number of observations on economic deprivation relative to previous affluence collected over forty years ago during the Great Depression of the 1930s (Eisenberg and Lazarsfeld 1938). These studies are often based on autobiographies and case histories. They lack a certain cohesiveness and precision, but nonetheless are chilling to read. Young children of the underpaid or unemployed may suffer a loss in peer group status. They may show emotional disturbances from losing the support of authority which deteriorated with the parents' financial situation. While young children regardless of social class prefer parents to play an active interventionist role in childcare (see Chapter 4 of this volume), parents affected by economic change may be physically and psychologically unavailable to their children (Greenley 1979). Without recognizing the complexities of the economic system and its relationship to the parents' resources, children lose both a measure of security and leadership. They have little or no target for ambition and commitment. The child's schoolwork suffers and, according to Eisenberg and Lazarsfeld (1938, p. 382), 'the younger children suffer more than the older probably because they are more dependent on their parents and have had less opportunity to build up resistance to catastrophic situations'.

For the older child, a crumbling parental authority may occur at the very time when it could have come to the aid of adolescent offspring who are troubled by the necessity to decide on a purposeful occupational identity of their own. To witness the parent's own difficulties in meeting the family's economic needs while still possessing the desire to attain material success could exasperate the child's identity crisis. The adolescent who is about to enter into adulthood without a parental target for commitment and ambition may be plagued by an acute feeling of becoming superfluous and aimless (Zawadski and Lazarsfeld 1935).

Recently reported longitudinal studies relevant to the relationship between economic deprivation and children's problem behaviour have systematically served to illuminate these early observations. This evidence, however, points to the importance of examining interactions involving other variables such as sex of child and the nature of the relationship between the parents.

Building on the earlier work of Elder (1974, 1979), Rockwell and Elder (1982) have investigated the relationship between deprivation and problem behaviour. Their subjects were born in 1928 and 1929 in Berkeley, California. About two-thirds were from families that were in the middle class during the Great Depression. The measure of deprivation was a loss in family income greater than 35 per cent during the period 1929–33. The data included two other sets of observations: the compatibility of the parental marriage in 1929, as indicated by ratings based on interviews with the husband and wife, and a measure of children's problem behaviour (Macfarlane, Allen, and Honzik 1954). The latter consisted of clinicians' ratings of reports provided by mothers during annual interviews on 35 different areas of problem behaviour when the children were 5–7, 8–10, and 11–13 years of age, including temper tantrums, stealing, and destructiveness.

The effects of economic change were significant for boys only, perhaps because the father's status as the family breadwinner was endangered and the father, as a primary role model for the son, may have had a greater effect on sons' social development and occupational aspirations than on daughters'. In the boys' case, weak marriages before the Depression were conducive to problem behaviour under conditions of economic deprivation. Boys from deprived, incompatible families fared worse than those from non-deprived incompatible ones. While some of these later grew up to be high achievers at age 40 during a time of postwar economic opportunity, the effects of deprivation may persist. As shown in a study of the subjects at middle age, consideration and resilience in the face of criticism were not seen to be among their assets (Elder and Rockwell 1979, p. 286). By contrast, boys from deprived families with strong marriages were rated as having the lowest levels of problem behaviour. Their scores were even lower than those of boys from non-deprived families headed by compatible parents. The deprived families appeared to have united forcefully in the face of difficult circumstances (Liker and Elder 1983). Their boys displayed little of the problem behaviour found elsewhere. Thus the relationship between economic deprivation and boys' problem behaviour is an indirect one in that it is mediated by parental conflict.

As Rockwell and Elder point out, these findings are beset with a number of problems; for example, mothers are not necessarily the most accurate observers of the behaviour of their children, particularly when they themselves are coping with the difficulties arising from economic decline. However, it must be emphasized that the data also have a unique advantage in that the children were non-clinical subjects observed during a time in history with a serious economic depression unequalled in this century. Moreover, while data specifically on children's perceptions of parents were not reported in this particular study, other studies suggest that conflict and family instability are associated with negative perceptions of the father (McCord, McCord, and Thurber 1963), and that boys who perceive their parents unfavourably are more likely to commit delinquent acts than those with favourable perceptions (Hirschi 1969; see Chapter 5).

Type B evidence

Measures of socioeconomic status (see, for example, Hollingshead 1957) cannot be fully equated with economic deprivation as defined by poverty relative to a general level of affluence in the community (type B); there are families who cannot be termed as deprived in an economic sense even though they are headed by persons with low levels of education or low occupational status. Still in this connection, the often observed relationship between socioeconomic status and juvenile delinquency is important and relevant (Simons 1978; Sutherland and Cressy 1974).

According to Gordon (1976, p. 201), 'one of the most thoroughly documented known crime and delinquency relationships is that with socioeconomic status'. Recently, however, this belief which had previously been widely acknowledged and accepted has come under attack (Emprey 1978; Tittle, Villemez, and Smith 1978). By this account there may be no relationship between social class and delinquency because those of low socioeconomic status are selectively arrested and prosecuted by the justice system. Self-reports of delinquency, as opposed to official crime statistics, indicate that a high proportion of all juveniles claim that they have engaged in delinquent activity and that there is no correlation between class and delinquency. At first glance, this argument seems persuasive enough. But it has met with a strong challenge mounted by Hindelang, Hirschi, and Weis (1979) who show that self-reports by their very nature concentrate primarily on relatively trivial offences such as drinking under age and skipping school. Serious offences have had to be eliminated from self-report studies because they were reported too infrequently by non-institutioned subjects. These include what many would conceive as the bread and butter of delinquent behaviour, for example, theft over $2, procurement of narcotics, and assault causing serious bodily injury. Not surprisingly, many juveniles of all classes admit to trivial offences rather than serious ones.

Self-report data on the incidence of serious delinquency behaviour is lacking and hence no conclusions may be drawn on this basis on the relationship between class and delinquency. But as Hindelang, Hirschi, and Weis (1979, p. 1011) point out, 'if we move to the point of incarceration where social class data on serious offenders are available, we find the substantial class differences assumed by traditional sociological theories'. Extremely serious crimes such as homicide may be difficult for any juveniles, regardless of social class, to commit undetected by the law. Given the very disproportionate rates of serious delinquency recorded in low socioeconomic status neighbourhoods, it would hardly seem appropriate to consign this phenomenon merely to a biased or faulty reporting system. Indeed, West (1982, p. 166) in an intensive longitudinal study of boys from a crowded working class area in London, found a close relationship between self-reported delinquency and official conviction records. Income was a better predictor of self-reported delinquency than was the father's occupation.

The socioeconomic status–delinquency relationship, as indicated by official crime statistics, has been consistently found and remains statistically significant even in an area so culturally homogeneous as Copenhagen, Denmark (McGarvey *et al.* 1981). As in the type A situation, this relationship may be mediated by children's perceptions of parents. In a study by Scheck and Emerick (1976), adolescent boys from two midwestern American cities were given a questionnaire designed to ascertain perceptions of childrearing practices used by their parents. Low parental socioeconomic status was found to be associated with low amounts of perceived parental support, control, and consistency. With regard to the relationship between childrearing and delinquency in predominantly low socioeconomic status families, McCord (1979) examined the records of boys aged 5–13 years who attended a treatment programme in Massachusetts during 1939–45 designed to prevent delinquency. The case records of these subjects, who came from families in which the father was primarily an unskilled worker, were coded for measures of childrearing (supervision of child, parental conflict, and the mother's affection). Thirty years later, information about criminal behaviour was taken from court records.

Childrearing variables accounted for a highly significant proportion of the variance in the total number of serious crimes for which the subjects had been convicted.

Studies discussed up to this point have been consistent with the thesis that economic deprivation is associated with children's problem behaviour, especially for boys under conditions in which there is conflict between the parents. However, the available evidence falls short of that required to interpret this association as a causal relationship. First, it may be that some third variable is implicated and that educational performance or IQ, for example, may make a contribution to children's problem behaviour which is independent of parental conflict or economic deprivation (*cf.* Moffitt *et al.* 1981). Second, the extent to which childrearing techniques, as distinct from economic deprivation, relates to problem behaviour remains to be determined as does the broad question of the direction of effect. Childrearing and behaviour may be mutual determinants of each other. Third, delinquents are a heterogeneous lot and a definitional problem exists for classification purposes (Schwartz and Johnson 1981). Differences across subgroups of delinquents have been shown to relate to family interaction patterns (Hetherington, Stouwie, and Ridberg 1971) and may relate to patterns of economic circumstances as well.

While studies to date suggest that economic deprivation is correlated with negative perceptions of parents which in turn is correlated with problem behaviour, the identification of causal connections among deprivation, perceptions, and behaviour awaits further longitudinal research. Perceptions and behaviour may be affected by many factors, for example, the age at which deprivation occurs, the reason for the deprivation, the length of the deprivation, and possibly the educational level of deprived family members. A distinction between unexpected and expected circumstances of deprivation could also be important. Unexpected deprivation might lead to greater conflict between the parents than if deprivation is expected (Becker, Landes, and Michael 1977, pp. 1160–1), thus affecting the parental image conveyed to children.

Particular attention as well should be given to processes by which children's perceptions are affected by the range of possible interactions among the mother, father, and child (*cf.* Parke, Power, and Gottman 1979). Negative perceptions of parents in a context of economic deprivation may be interpreted in terms of a loss in stature of the father relative to the mother. In discussing the circumstances of deprivation on children of the Great Depression, Elder (1974, pp. 100–1) points out that when the father was unemployed, mother dominance of decisions affecting the family's welfare did not so much damage the image of the father as increase positive evaluations of the mother. Similarly, in the modern working-class family, maternal employment can be met with disapproval from the father often accompanied by the belief that the mother's working signifies an inability on his part to provide. In both instances, a more enhanced image of the mother in the son's eyes, elevating the mother above the father in relative adulation, may give rise to father–son tension and contribute to problem behaviour. This issue is re-examined in Chapters 6 and 8.

Case number 2: Economic deprivation, psychological well-being, and child abuse

A second relationship between economic deprivation and the quality of parent–child relations is between deprivation, adult psychological wellbeing, and child abuse and neglect.

It has long been observed that the self-perceptions of adults are influenced by their work experience (Kohn and Schooler 1978). Clearly, a sense of personal competence and self-efficacy is defined and reinforced by having a role in the economy (Gurney 1980). Employment can give purpose and structure to behaviour outside the work setting (M. Jahoda 1979, 1981). A parent gains status, authority, and generativity, a 'concern for establishing and guiding the next generation' (Erikson 1968, p. 138). A longitudinal study by Mortimer and Lorence (1979) has shown that an individual's sense of competence is strongly influenced by the challenge, the amount of innovative thinking, and the degree of decision-making latitude involved in work. Moreover, surveys of overall life satisfaction in the United States have shown perceived financial success to be central to adults' self-definition (Campbell, Converse, and Rodgers 1976).

Adult mental health and economic deprivation (Types A and B)

Economically deprived adults may lack this sense of competence and self-definition. A recent University of Illinois study surveyed 1507 English-speaking civilians above the age of 18 (Smith and Kluegel 1982). Respondents were asked, 'Generally speaking, would you consider yourself/your own household today to be poor, just able to get along, comfortable, prosperous, or rich?' Then they were asked to say whether their current standard of living could be attributed to 'internal' factors such as education, ability, or effort or 'external' factors over which an individual has less control such as good or bad luck or as being helped or held back by other people. In addition, amongst other measures of affect, subjects were asked to rate whether they feel worried almost always, just sometimes, or almost never. Perceived worriedness was greater amongst those who rated themselves as poor and who attributed their poverty to external factors, presumably because these 'poor' see themselves to be at the mercy of undesirable trickle-down influences.

The extreme situation is the case of persons who have experienced involuntary long-term unemployment owing to circumstances beyond their control. Unemployment is often accompanied by a significant propensity toward mental illness, depression, and even suicide (Dooley and Catalano 1980; Shepherd 1981). Hepworth (1980) examined the mental health and psychological wellbeing of five groups of unemployed workers (managerial, white-collar, skilled, semi-skilled, and unskilled) on the Government Unemployment Registrar in Sheffield, England. Length of unemployment was associated with self-reports of dissatisfaction with present-life circumstances on the General Health Questionnaire (Goldberg 1972). The degree to which an unemployed man felt his time was occupied correlated significantly with occupational status and was the best predictor of mental health. A longitudinal study by Banks and Jackson (1982) indicates that the experience of unemployment is more likely to create psychiatric symptoms rather than the reverse.

Economic deprivation may also trickle down to lower the worth of children to parents. By far the most blatant and extreme illustration of the effects of deprivation on parents' relationships with children comes from the high incidence of child abuse in poor families. It is true that cases of child abuse and neglect are known in all socioeconomic classes and that two socioeconomically similar neighbourhoods may have different rates of abuse and neglect, depending on the availability of 'support systems' (Garbarino and Sherman 1980). Nevertheless, such cases do predominate in lower-class families and these families are particularly prone to mental health disorders associated with economic strain. Hepworth's (1980) data clearly indicate that unemployed semi-skilled and unskilled workers have a poorer psychological wellbeing than those unemployed of a higher occupational status. This result is in line with the consistent finding that stressful life events more adversely affect the mental health of lower social class individuals (Brown, Bhrolchain, and Harris 1975; Sandler and Block 1979). According to the model offered by Wheaton (1980) on the basis of two longitudinal studies of stressful life changes, the employment status and deference behaviour of low socioeconomic status individuals suggests to these persons that they are less than averagely successful and that they have little personal power. This fatalism undermines the ability to cope in stressful situations and results in a vulnerability to psychological disorder related to low socioeconomic status.

In the case of young mothers, poor psychological wellbeing is related to stressful life events, especially low income or unpredictability of income (Belle 1980). In an intensive study of 42 low income Boston mothers, such stressful conditions were seen to be associated with mutually unfavourable perceptions held by mothers and children, less supportive behaviour from the mother to the child, and more negative behaviour in the home on the part of the child (Zelkowitz *et al.* 1979).

Child abuse and economic deprivation

Type B evidence

Psychological wellbeing is negatively affected by economic deprivation associated with loss of employment or low socioeconomic status. By the same token, Pelton (1978) has shown that, although poor people are more subject to public scrutiny, the relationship between poverty and child abuse and neglect may not merely be assigned to a faulty reporting system which monitors the poor and not the rich. Even looking at only impoverished families, the greatest child neglect occurs in the poorest of the poor (Gil 1971, p. 640; Giovannoni and Billingsley 1970).

Perhaps there is no better single example of the importance of studying the socioeconomic conditions underlying parent–child relations than child abuse. Pelton charges that to indulge in a myth of classlessness is to reinforce the interests of middle-class professionals who maintain that abuse is a medical problem rather than a poverty problem. Ultimately, this myth serves to divert efforts away from alleviating poverty to supporting a prestigious and glamorous medical model. It assumes a reductionist explanation that abuse is a result of weakly controlled parental impulses whose psychological symptoms can be traced back to biological dysfunctions controllable by drugs. But to implement more forceful and direct measures to eliminate a possible major antecedent of child abuse, connections between economic strain and deteriorating family relations must be recognized. Because child abuse occurs more frequently under conditions of economic hardship, it cannot be simply 'medicalized' and interpreted in terms of mechanistic, biological processes.

Type A evidence

Many observers have noted a relationship between child abuse and economic strain (Garbarino and Crouter 1978; Gil 1971; Light 1973). But again the problem arises of inferring causal direction on the basis of correlational data, and the third variable explanation has remained a plausible alternative to one involving economic deprivation. In an important step toward resolving the issue, Steinberg, Catalano, and Dooley (1981) have used a longitudinal approach to test the hypothesis that undesirable economic change leads to increased child abuse. Their data come from Los Angeles and Orange Counties in California and were analysed over a 30-month period. Correlational analyses across time indicated that periods of contraction in the work force (in other words, high job loss) are followed by a significant increase in child abuse.

Since this result occurred in both communities, it is unlikely that non-economic variables associated with a unique time and place, rather than workforce decline, lead to increases in child abuse. But as Steinberg *et al.* do point out, another alternative explanation is logically conceivable (though perhaps somewhat far fetched and certainly no more plausible than the economic stress one): workforce changes precede changes in reported child abuse while the actual rate of child abuse remains constant.

More accurate estimates of the true incidence of abuse merit attention, possibly through repeated epidemiological surveys. However, as for the relationship between social class and children's serious problem behaviour, a strong association exists between social class and extremely serious instances of child abuse, which presumably could not go undetected regardless of class (Nixon *et al.* 1981). Coronial reports and inquest files in the state of Queensland, Australia (population 2 million), over the period 1968–79, indicate that in all 22 cases where a child under 5 years died as a result of adult-inflicted non-accidental injuries, the family was from a lower socioeconomic group.

Implications

In examining the effects on the microsystem at Stage 7 of a trickle-down model, conclusive proof is lacking that economic change and deprivation is a primary cause of deteriorating parent–child relations. The true incidence of all cases of problem behaviour, delinquency, and child abuse—trivial, substantial, and serious—can only be estimated. A cause-and-effect relationship which rules out all third variable explanations would be, in any event, exceedingly difficult to establish. Moreover, definitions of economic deprivation (both types) may mask important subgroups of deprived, and data are largely lacking, for example, on the issue of whether deprivation affects the quality of parent–child relations in predominantly deprived families of low educational achievement.

However, there is sufficient evidence to suggest that connections between deprivation and the quality of parent–child relations in some circumstances, especially those of serious cases of delinquency and child abuse which do not usually remain undetected, are entirely plausible and a distinct possibility. Apart from non-economic forces, difficult economic conditions stemming from an application or misapplication of trickle-down policy may diminish children's perceptions of their parents, exacerbating conflict already present in the family and giving rise to problem behaviour in boys. In times of economic strain, there may be an increase in the incidence of child abuse or neglect.

Possible relationships between the two cases can be noted. In the context of deprivation, parents may not be as available to their children for physical and psychological support. Mothers' mental health may be affected by work and financial demands which reduce their ability to deal with situations involving the child (Warr and Parry 1982, p. 501). Since children highly appraise a sensitivity to situations (see Chapter 4 of this volume), their perceptions of the mother may become unfavourable. Children and parents may point to each other as scapegoats for a perceived inadequacy to meet family responsibilities. It is as if, battered by economic forces,

> We cannot stop struggling forward.
> Because we are not salmon, we cannot die
>   when the children are born.
> Because we are not bears, we cannot go off
> When the children are raised . . .

Strung out one by one, we move together
through the landscape. Children and parents
(Wayman 1973, p. 82)

Ahead

We have just examined some of the interactions between the workplace and the family, as well as higher-order effects from more
remote environmental sources such as economic recession which
transform the parents' occupational role indirectly affecting children's development. According to the Bronfenbrenner (1979)
model, these interrelations are located within the mesosystem and,
by extension, the exosystem. Both comprise networks of relations
between groups and institutions which encompass the developing
child and exert indirect, though powerful, effects at particular points
in time; for example, the pressure on the parent of long working
hours and extensive travel as it directly relates to marital stability
and the neighbourhood and indirectly relates to the child (Aberle
and Naegele 1952; Renshaw 1976).

Toward a more complete account, attention must turn now to the
'microsystem', the complex of direct relations between the child and
the immediate home setting, more specifically between children's
behaviour and their perception of others. Chapter 2 is devoted to an
examination of children's perceptions as these relate to moral development, and Chapter 3 to how these relate to the development of
intellectual performance. In both chapters, consideration will be
given to sex differences in children's perceptions of the self in relation to parental attributes and expectations.

Chapter 4 looks at the child's perceptions of parents' roles and
responsibilities as moderated by peer-group influences. Chapter 5
examines the relation between perceptions and children's orientations toward the law and matters of criminal justice. Chapter 6
turns to children's orientations toward achievement and matters of
economic justice.

Then many of the issues raised in the first chapter are taken up
again in Chapters 7 and 8. Chapter 7 is concerned with the question
of whether development is spurred on by children's experience of
cognitive conflict or conflict with parents and peers. Chapter 8
returns to the exosystem in considering children's understanding of
parenthood as influenced by the socioeconomic context. It deals
with what Bronfenbrenner has termed the 'macrosystem', the over-
arching cultural and ideological patterns of society of which the

microsystems, mesosystems, and exosystems are concrete manifestations. It also discusses the roles of mothers and fathers and the child as a priority in contemporary Western society. Toward an integrative, developmental model, reciprocal influences between parent–child relations and the socioeconomic environment will be explored. From the standpoint of a developmental psychology set in the context of a changing society (Belsky 1981; Peele 1981; Putnam 1973; Sampson 1981), the aim will be to connect the complexity of parent–child relations with social and economic events.

2

Moral development in context

Certainly the most notable approach to moral development in recent years has been that taken by Lawrence Kohlberg (1969, 1976, 1978). Stimulated by the work of the Swiss psychologist Jean Piaget, particularly in his book *The moral judgement of the child* (1977*b*) Kohlberg has proposed that moral development is marked by a sequence of cognitive stages which characterize the development of reasoning about moral dilemmas. In young children, moral reasoning is said to be oriented first toward punishment and obedience. With increasing age, individuals proceed through stages in which reasoning becomes oriented toward instrumental hedonism, then mutual interpersonal expectations, law and order, and finally ethical principles which are upheld despite the conventions of the majority.

The moral dilemma about 'Heinz and the drug' is often used by Kohlberg (1969, p. 379) to illustrate the existence of stages:

In Europe, a woman was near death from cancer. One drug might save her, a form of radium that a druggist in the same town had recently discovered. The druggist was charging $2000, ten times what the drug cost him to make. The sick woman's husband, Heinz, went to everyone he knew to borrow the money, but he could only get together about half of what it cost. He told the druggist that his wife was dying and asked him to sell it cheaper or let him pay later. But the druggist said, 'No'. The husband got desperate and broke into the man's store to steal the drug for his wife. Should the husband have done that? Why?

In response to this hypothetical dilemma, young children not surprisingly see a resolution in terms of whether or not Heinz is likely to get caught and punished for stealing, or whether or not his wife would be angry at him for his decision. Older adolescents and adults are more likely to view Heinz's actions in terms of abstract issues or principles concerning the rights of life and property and the role of the state in enforcing laws.

Support for Kohlberg's cognitive-developmental stage model has been found in a 20-year longitudinal study of boys' moral judgement by Colby *et al.* (1983). The subjects were 50 boys from two Chicago suburban areas, one predominantly upper-middle class, the other predominantly lower-middle and working class. The study consisted of six testing times in which Kohlberg's moral dilemmas were administered at 3–4 year intervals. The boys proceeded through the stages in the hypothesized sequence with no subject reported as skipping a stage and with a negligible number moving from a higher stage to a lower one.

But no approach to the study of moral development is at all satisfactory unless it deals with behaviour. Individuals at a principled stage of moral reasoning on Kohlberg's hypothetical dilemmas may actually behave no differently than those at lower stages. They may, for example, be largely indistinguishable in their sharing, helping, stealing, and lying. Recently a series of reviews has dealt with the relationship between moral behaviour, on the one hand, and Kohlberg-type cognitive measures of moral reasoning and perspective-taking on the other (Blasi 1980; Jurkovic 1980; Underwood and Moore 1982). All have arrived at the conclusion that there is generally a statistically significant relationship between cognition and behaviour, though this varies in strength according to the nature of the measures and behaviours studied. However, the magnitude of the relationship is usually meagre to modest, often accounting for only 10–15 per cent of the variance in behaviour.

This pattern of results can be explained in a number of ways. It may be, for example, that the cognitive measures such as Kohlberg's are at an early stage of development and have not yet been fully refined to take account of the diversity and multidimensional nature of moral reasoning and perspective-taking shown in everyday situations (Ford 1979; Houssaidas and Brown 1980; Kurdek 1978, Rubin 1978, Rubin and Trotter 1977; Yussen 1977). In the case of adult moral development, judgements of responsibility together with the construct of substages may prove to provide a more satisfactory link between moral reasoning and behaviour (Candee and Kohlberg 1982). Alternatively, it has been pointed out that cognitive measures, however refined, might ultimately account for only a part (though a modestly significant one) of the variation in manifest moral behaviour. According to Jurkovic, for example, predictability might be improved if more attention were to be devoted to personality and motivational factors. According to Blasi, behavioural predictions would be enhanced if cognitive-developmental theory were to be integrated with the self and related constructs such as self-definition. From the viewpoint of social learning theory as well, 'self-phenomena often function as the most immediate determinants of behaviour'; even so, 'self-processes have yet to receive the systematic attention in psychological theorizing and attention they deserve' (Bandura 1982, p. 33). It should be noted that this approach does not deny the validity of moral reasoning for, as Saltzstein (1983, p. 114) has recently reiterated, moral stages stand on their own and do 'not determine the action decision but the reasons for deciding'.

The notion that measures of self-definition could contribute to a sounder basis for predicting overt behaviour gives rise to the purpose of this chapter: to examine children's self-definition in relation to others. First, this will involve a consideration of the concept of identification. For above all, identification, while provocative and controversial, historically has been germane and central to the question of self-definition in social and personality development. Second, children's self-definition, which has been construed as a form of identification, will be examined as an antecedent and a consequent of rule-guided behaviour. The objective is to provide a more concrete basis for accurate behavioural predictions in both girls and boys.

A renewed look at identification as a developmental process seems timely for two reasons. First, as recognition has grown of the importance of connecting cognitive and developmental processes to social and historical conditions which interact with the family environment, it has become increasingly clear that cognitive measures of moral reasoning are most relevant to behavioural situations in which carefully considered moral judgements can be made. As Krebs and Rosenwald (1977, p. 86) have pointed out, these situations often involve 'low-key unemotional conflicts', and cognitive measures, such as those of Kohlberg, 'would not be expected to predict impulsive behaviours that are minimally mediated by cognitive processes as well, including many of the behaviours commonly considered most moral and immoral, like acts of heroism, rape and murder'. Second, recent studies have demonstrated that many processes researched in experimental psychology are in the realm of the 'unconscious' (Shevrin and Dickman 1980) and that affect may precede and be independent of cognition (Fiske 1981; Zajonc 1984). At least to this extent, even the version of identification as an unconscious, affect-laden desire to be like significant others would, in principle, seem no less worthy of empirical attention than unconscious processes studied in perception or physiological psychology.

Self-definition and identification

The Freudian account

According to Freud (1961*a*, 1961*b*), identification has a biological and evolutionary root. During prehistoric times, the father within the primal horde chased the sons away in order to possess all the women for himself. Disobedience was punished by castration. At last, the sons acted together to kill the father. To maintain security and ensure the survival of human society the sons relinquished the conquered women as objects of gratification and enacted incest taboos. These were handed down from generation to generation. The defence mechanism of identification evolved so that castration anxiety could be reduced. The energy addressed toward possessing objects of gratification and displacing barriers to attaining objects was redirected. The boy unconsciously identifies both with his mother as a source of love which can be lost (anaclitic identification) and more importantly with his father's powerful authority (aggressive identification). Both forms of identification are narcissistic in so far as the child internalizes the representations of nurturance and power in his superego. The Oedipus complex of the male child, a desire to overthrow the father and possess the mother, gives way to a sense of guilt and conscience against causing injury to his parents. The boy's adoption of lofty moral positions is linked to a strong, potentially very punishing, superego which is achieved primarily through aggressive identification (Freud 1961*b*).

Freud was comparatively unclear about the psychology of women. He surmised that the anxiety of girls during the phallic stage results primarily in anaclitic identification. When the girl notices that boys have a penis, an organ which she lacks and thus envies, she turns to her father for gratification. For her desire to possess the father, she fears punishment by the mother, not by castrastion since she has 'already been castrated', but by loss of love. Freud speculated that the female Oedipus complex is resolved by relinquishing the father and incorporating the personality characteristics of her parents (particularly the mother) into her own personality. Once again this sex role development leads to the internalization of parents' moral positions. However, the girl fails to equal the level of conscience development attained by the boy because her identification is anaclitic rather than aggressive in nature.

Freud regarded identification as a defence mechanism buried deeply within the 'hot-core' of the psyche. Such ideas are not easily tested since they are based on the assumption that personality is rooted in the unconscious and that unconscious phenomena can only be indirectly inferred from overt and often pathological behaviour. Evidence for psychoanalytic concepts and complexes frequently comes not from systematic experimentation and observation but from case studies and anecdotes (see, for example, Bettleheim 1943). In view of this quandary, Freud's theory cannot at the moment be regarded as scientific, for scientific theories have a degree of precision and determinateness which allow them to be verified or falsified. In this connection, Freud's own theoretical vacillation certainly does not help. For example, within one paragraph he asserts that a child's very strict conscience may be independent of his child-rearing, may be 'determined by the amount of punitive aggression he receives from his father', and at the same time can be acquired through a lenient upbringing (Freud 1961a, p. 77).

Derivatives from the Freudian account

However, it would be a mistake to dismiss psychoanalytic theory as a doctrine of faith or as merely interesting mythology. As Farrell (1981) has written, Freud's theory may represent an 'empirical speculative synthesis' which is years in advance of the availability of supporting or disconfirming proof. In the 1950s psychologists were often hospitable toward this view, and the decade of the 1950s might be regarded as the golden age of identification. Indeed, without going into precise details as to the definition of identification, Foote (1951) was able to proclaim that:

Faith in one's conception of one's self is the key which unlocks the physiological resources of the human organism to perform the initiated act. Doubt of identity, or confusion, where it does not cause complete disorientation, certainly drains action of its meaning, and thus limits mobilization of the organic correlates of emotion, drive and energy which constitute the introspectively sensed 'push' of motivated action (p. 486). . . . Without the binding thread of identity one could not evaluate the succession of situations. Literally, one could say there would be no value in living, since value only exists or occurs relative to particular identities. . . . Moreover, it is only through identification as the sharing of identity that individual motives become social values and social values, individual motives (p. 487).

Without being able to describe how 'one acquires, and gets committed to particular identities', Foote nevertheless regarded identification as *the* basis for a theory of motivation. In the years to follow, efforts continued to clarify the antecedents, motivations, and behavioural outcomes involved in identification toward paving the way for empirical verification.

However, partly in exasperation as to the vagueness of what is meant by 'identification', there were those who maintained that the term should be reserved for only certain restricted types of phenomena or even dropped altogether. Identification was reworked by learning theorists focusing attention on aspects of reinforcement and imitation in parent–child relations. For example, in pulling away from the biological and evolutionary basis for Freudian identification and the notion of an Oedipus complex, Mowrer (1950, 1953) suggested several environmental explanations for cross-generational similarity in behaviour including the affection and power of the person with whom identification is attempted. He reversed Freud's sequence in which identification preceded the child's emotional tie to the parent. According to Mowrer, a learned love for a parent determines the object choice for gratification, and not the other way around. Sears (1957) viewed identification as 'acting like another person'. It was portrayed as a process which varies positively with the amount of affectionate nurture given the child, with the severity of the demands placed on the child by the mother, with the extent to which the mother uses withdrawal of love as a discipline technique, and with the degree to which the person with whom the child identifies is absent. Sears also restated many psychoanalytic ideas in learning theory terminology but, like Freud, saw a special role for the mother and regarded the outcome of identification as a generalized pattern of imitation. By contrast, Sanford (1955) went so far as to claim that parental reward and punishment directly reinforces behaviour and that behaviour conforming to parental rules and standards can be explained without resorting to any mediating notion of 'identification' or 'internalization'.

Several others held a more charitable outlook on identification as an explanatory concept. Like Foote, these theorists took a cognitive or 'symbolic interactionist' approach to parent–child relations. For example, Kagan (1958) defined identification as an acquired *cognitive* response within a person oriented toward two affective goal states: mastery of the environment and love and affection. According to Kagan, a motive for identification resides in the child's *perceptions* (accurate or exaggerated) of an adult model's command of the child's goal states. A boy's desire to identify with the father and command the attractive goals which the father possesses will give rise to an important consequence of this identification: an attempt to take on what are perceived to be the father's characteristics as often evidenced in sex-typed behaviour (Kagan 1964). While the content of identification as an acquired cognitive response can consist of similarity in overt behaviour between an individual and a model, such matched behaviour is not an all-or-none process and outward similarity may mask different motives underlying behaviour.

Working closely to the Freudian distinction between aggressive and anaclitic identification, Slater (1961) sought to dispel the notion that much identification is as a result of a resolution of the Oedipal situation. He drew a dichotomy separating 'personal identification' motivated primarily out of love and admiration from a 'positional identification' motivated out of fear and envy. For Slater, positional identification occurs only in so far as personal identification fails to develop. As in Kagan's account, identification is cognitive in that it is dependent on the degree to which the object commands desired goal states. There is a 'generalized similarity' between the child and either parent regardless of sex.

Finally, Bronfenbrenner (1960) explored three broad classes of phenomena for which the term identification has been used: (1) as behaviour, (2) as motivation, and (3) as process. Identification in the first sense emphasizes (though not exclusively) imitation of a model and matching responses. The second refers to a disposition to act like another. Since this disposition arises from the child's subjective perception of a model's behaviour, it may be distorted or exaggerated. Third, identification may be viewed in terms of the process by which children come to emulate a model either by learning through reward and punishment or by anaclitic and aggressive mechanisms. This process embraces the relationship between motivation and behaviour.

Identification in terms of the social learning and cognitive-developmental approaches

As the preceding writers have all recognized in one way or another, the confusion over identification certainly stems from the work of Freud himself. Mowrer (1950, pp. 582–5) went to some lengths to delineate three of the guises in which Freud used the term 'identification' in his ongoing revisions of psychoanalytic theory. First, identification was simply equated with imitation. Second, we have identification as narcissism. This is perhaps the most cognitive of the three ways in which Freud used the term. Narcissistic identification is not a desire or motivation to adopt as one's own the rules and standards of others. Rather, it involves a perception that others have attributes which are similar to those one already possesses which gives rise to a desire to identify with persons who are perceived to have similar characteristics. According to Mowrer, this second sense in which Freud employed the term identification 'probably has no enduring theoretical significance' and stands in contrast to the 'third and most instructive sense': identification as a motive to be like others outside oneself which allows the individual to measure his or her behaviour by an ego-ideal arising from perceptions of valued others.

The importance of identification as a motive in Freud's third sense of the term was acknowledged by Mowrer, Bronfenbrenner, and others. But it was hardly surprising that theoretical expositions in the 1960s distanced themselves away from this pivotal element in psychoanalytic theory for, at the very least, it was apparent to many that the concept of identification had become 'hopelessly entangled in semantics' (Bandura 1969, p. 218). The result was to catch all accounts of identification in the same net. On the one hand, social learning theorists preferred to deal with identification only in Freud's first sense of the term which employed identification interchangeably with imitation rather than with questions pertaining to identification in the other two senses, questions regarding self-definition and motivation. On the other hand, followers of Kohlberg's cognitive-developmental approach did not completely dismiss the possibility of identification as motive but centred on identification defined as similarity to others: that is, a recognition and preference for those possessing similar attributes such as masculinity. For Kohlberg, aspects of cognitive development determine identificatory or similarity behaviour which takes on a generalized pattern and may occur in the absence of a model. Internalization, the self-acceptance of moral values and adult behavioural standards in the absence of external authority, is mainly a result of cognitive development such as gender constancy, the knowledge that one's gender is fixed and that boys become fathers and girls mothers: 'Accordingly, our view is that identifications do not cause moral (or sex-role) internalization but develop in parallel with them, and help to support moral or sex-role attitudes. Cognitive-developmental changes in conceptions of moral rules and social sex-roles are causative forces in the formation of parent identifications as much or more than the reverse' (Kohlberg 1969, p. 428). Correlations between sex-typing and identification with the same sex parent are seen as 'primarily resulting from the tendency for boys high on masculine sex-typing to identify with the father rather than for a high father-identification to cause masculine typing' (Kohlberg 1966, p. 127). A desire to play masculine roles leads to a striving for power and control of the environment. It might be noted that the description of identification as similarity behaviour is relevant to the Freudian sense of identification as narcissistic.

By this account, no special role for parental identification is assumed and identification is relegated to being only part of a much broader account of imitative processes in general. According to Kohlberg (1969, p. 471), 'a specific relation to a specific good parent is neither necessary nor sufficient for normal or advanced moral development, since father absence, father's moral level, and the "good" child-rearing techniques, however defined, do not predict to such maturity'. Since then this position has been reaffirmed in that only a weak to modest relationship appears to exist between parents' and boys' responses on Kohlberg's moral dilemma measures. Despite the particular importance of family in girls' perceptions of the social self as shown by their spontaneous self-descriptions (McGuire and McGuire 1982), correlations between parents' and girls' responses are negligible (Haan, Langer, and Kohlberg 1976).

Identification is viewed by Kohlberg to be similar to moral reasoning in that both have a cognitive basis. In common with Kagan (1958, 1964) and White (1959), mastery of the environment is regarded as the impetus for an imitation which is followed by an identification with a competent model. A realization of shared similarity with others, often developed through role-taking and social interaction, also gives rise to imitation and identification. However, unlike Kagan's formulation, the love and affection of a specific parent does not present an important goal state for identification as a motive.

Identification is thus a by-product or offshoot of imitation and has only a subsidiary supporting role in a cognitive-developmental account of moral development. Similarly, affect is defined in terms of the child's cognitive development (Kohlberg 1969, p. 393):

Our point of view is that the 'cognitive' definition of the moral situation directly determines the moral emotion which the situation arouses. Cognitive-developmental stages, both non-moral and moral, are stimulated through 'cognitive conflict'. Exposure to conflicting reasoning at a high stage adjacent to that used by an individual provides the required impetus to propel changes in a person's cognitive structures.

Five assumptions, at least, are present in Kohlberg's description of a cognitive-developmental approach to socialization: (1) that cognitive development and role-taking abilities are a necessary though not sufficient basis for the development of moral reasoning; (2) that cognition moulds affect; (3) that the vehicle underlying development to higher cognitive stages of moral reasoning is conflict between cognitions; (4) that identification shows no direction relation with moral behaviour but may serve to contribute (in ways not precisely specified) to the behavioural outcome of moral cognitions; and (5) that there are no sex differences in moral reasoning apart from those which relate to occupation and education. While many of Kohlberg's claims rest on material which remains unpublished and hence of unknown quality, these issues can be reappraised with respect to the research findings of the 1970s and early 1980s.

Cognitive development and role-taking—a necessary but not sufficient basis for moral development Kohlberg (1969, 1976) claimed that cognitive development is a necessary but not sufficient condition for the development of role-taking ability which in turn is necessary but not sufficient for moral reasoning development. This assertion has met with varying degrees of support from role-taking tasks in which subjects are asked to describe situations from divergent viewpoints. These have consisted of spatial measures in which the task, for example, involves distinguishing left from right or hypothetical situations in which the task is to describe the information possessed by different story characters. Aside from Haan, Weiss, and Johnson (1982) who found no association for women and a significant but low association for men, most studies point to a substantial association between cognitive ability, role-taking and the development of moral reasoning. Yet there is inconclusive support for the necessary but not sufficient proposition (Keasey 1975; Krebs and Gillmore 1982; Kuhn *et al.* 1977). Role-taking, for young children in particular, appears not to be a necessary prerequisite for reasoning at higher moral stages. Krebs and Gillmore (1982) found evidence for the necessary but not sufficient proposition to be strongest for older children as shown by the ability to comprehend that another person can think about them thinking about him or her. However, for younger children aged about 5 years, higher stage reasoning was not contingent upon role-taking as shown by the simple ability to adopt another person's perspective. Moreover, the recently longitudinal study of males' moral reasoning supporting the validity of Kohlberg's stages (Colby *et al*. 1983) began at age 10 and does not address the question of developmental changes in the moral development of young children. The work reviewed in Chapter 4 of this volume suggests that an implicit theory of the intentions underlying others' behaviour is present early in the child's development and does not develop in a sequence paralleling that in the development of moral reasoning.

Cognition determines affect   As mentioned earlier, recent research using adult subjects suggests that affect and cognition may exist independently of one another, and that affect precedes cognition rather than the reverse. If cognitive-developmental stages are neither a necessary nor sufficient edifice for moral reasoning, affect might be assumed to play a more important role. This is not to deny that affect and cognition are interrelated in moral behaviour (Dienstbier *et al*. 1975), but that certain cognitions are more affect-laden than others and that these may serve as antecedents for manifest moral behaviour. As will be seen, verbal self-reports of identification (that is, self-definition in relation to others) may be an apt indication of such 'hot' affect-laden cognition, more so than 'cool' role-taking tasks used by those working from Kohlberg's cognitive-developmental approach.

Conflict between cognitions   The idea that development is a result of exposure to reasoning at higher and conflicting stages of moral development was first mooted by Piaget and adopted by Kohlberg (1969, p. 407; Kohlberg and Turiel 1971). However, research by Blatt and Kohlberg (1975) and Turiel (1966) claiming that moral reasoning development can be stimulated in this way remains controversial (Kurtines and Greif 1974; Elkind and Weiner 1978). On the contrary, in the related domain of cognitive development, studies reviewed in Chapter 7 of this volume indicate that development is stimulated more by agreement than by inducing conflict. If this is the case for cognitive development, it certainly might apply to a cognitive-developmental account of moral reasoning as well. Indeed, conflict may impede, rather than stimulate, moral reasoning about issues of distributive justice (Damon and Killen 1982). Consistent with an identification account, development may be stimulated more by agreement rather than conflict between the moral orientations of the child and significant others.

There is no direct relation between identification and moral development For Kohlberg (1969), 'measures of identification do not correlate well with one another' (p. 470) and, 'from the cognitive-developmental viewpoint ... it is impossible to conceive of such basic and near universal features of personality development as morality as being directly caused by parent identification. There are too many developmental and cultural forces tending to produce "normal" morality to see these attitudes as contingent on special unique relationships to parents' (p. 428). Moreover, ' "moral values" or attitudes conceived as affective quanta in the usual social attitude sense do not predict directly to behaviour in conflict situations' (p. 394).

The lack of a substantial, direct relationship between the moral reasoning of parents and children would seem to fly in the face of a wealth of common-sense observation as far back as Aristotle. Contrary to Kohlberg, there are indications that a direct relationship does exist between children's perceptions of their parents and manifest moral behaviour. For example, Bixenstine, DeCorte, and Bixenstine (1976) found that children's expressed willingness to engage in peer-endorsed misbehaviour was significantly correlated with a loss in favourableness toward parents. By contrast, cognitive measures of moral judgement seem insensitive to this type of conformity behaviour at least when Kohlberg's global scoring system is used (Blasi 1980, p. 37; Santrock 1975).

Furthermore, it is apparent that the general cognitive structure underlying moral development may be no more unified than measures of identification. Despite revisions to the scoring method which have succeeded in eliminating some response variability, substantial variability still exists, particularly for preadolescents (Colby *et al.* 1983, p. 23; Cortese 1984; Fischer 1983). At age 10 the alternative form correlation between form A and B of the Kohlberg measures is a non-significant 0.37 ($n = 19$). Unlike for older age groups, the correlations between moral judgement scores at age 10 and those at later ages, though significant, are not very high (Colby *et al.* 1983, p. 51). Thus it does seem unfair to assert that self-definition through identification, even if measured by an albeit somewhat fragmented index of attitudes and personality, cannot lead directly to any theoretically meaningful predictions in young children. Theories of identification and their derivates have all dwelt on the intricacies of identificatory processes, about *different* generalized motives and about *different* general patterns of behaviour, rather than on identification as a global entity.

Sex differences in moral reasoning?   Whether there are sex differences in moral reasoning when educational and occupational background are controlled is highly controversial (Bussey and Maughan 1982; Gilligan 1982; Lyons 1983; Rest 1983). Plainly there are sex differences in moral behaviour within children of the same social background especially with regard to honesty and delinquency (Rutter and Giller 1983). Sex differences also emerge with regard to empathy with females displaying more empathic concern than males on self-reports of concern for the distress of others (Eisenberg and Lennon 1983 p. 125; Hoffman 1977).

The insensitivity of cognitive measures of moral reasoning to sex differences may lead to inaccurate behavioural predictions. Kohlberg (1966, p. 124) himself has described 'the developmental mechanisms of identification in girls' as 'much more complex and ambiguous' than in boys and the most definitive longitudinal research derived from the Kohlberg approach has been based on a sample of 58 boys (Colby *et al.* 1983). According to Gilligan (1982), females construct solutions to moral problems out of a morality of caring, connections, and relationships, while the male approach involves a morality of rights, personal autonomy, and categories. The thesis of Chodorow (1978) and Gilligan (1982, pp. 7–8; Lyons 1983) implies that a close, caring identificatory relationship with significant others, particularly the mother, should precede girls' rule-guided behaviour especially in situations of compliance to the rules where a selfless connectedness is expected. By contrast, following Kohlberg, a sex-typed personal autonomy in boys implies an individual separateness and flaunting of behavioural rules which should precede an identification with the father. Indeed, to date, the slender support for Kohlberg's position that sex-role conceptions such as gender constancy are linked with sex-appropriate behaviour comes from data on males. As Huston (1983, p. 409) has remarked, 'There is some tendency for children with high gender constancy to be more attentive to, or influenced by, same-sex models, as evidenced in a series of studies using televised stimuli ... but the findings are inconsistent and occur primarily for boys'.

Cognitive identification in relation to moral behaviour

All of this amounts to the proposition that some form or forms of identification, if properly delineated, cannot be ruled out as central and pervasive in the behavioural aspects of moral development, especially for young children and adolescent girls. Evidence exists which is both consistent and anomalous with the cognitive-developmental approach. While cognitive measures of moral reasoning and perspective-taking have fallen short of powerful behavioural predictions, the reasoning–behaviour link is seen to be strongest for older subjects at the higher stages (Candee and Kohlberg 1982). The possibility remains that, for young children, measures of identification as self defined in terms of the attributes of significant others might still serve to tap an affect-laden 'hot cognition' which predicts rule-guided behaviour.

Identification in the young child may be reflected in the verbally expressed desire to be like the parent and adopt his or her rules or standards for behaviour. For older children or adolescents, identification may reflect the recognition that a parent has attributes which they already possess. Since rules and standards for behaviour are perceived to be shared by parent and child, these are emulated in a narcissistic fashion.

In two ways, the social-cognitive identification approach departs from that of Freud. In the first place it skirts around the Oedipus complex and has no necessary connection with evolutionary, biological accounts of identification. It is the case, as Stoke (1950, p. 228) aptly remarked many years ago, that to 'Freudians, identification without the Oedipus complex would be as strange as Hamlet without the "gloomy Dane"'. Nevertheless, as philosophers of science have often pointed out, frequently a hazy, speculative concept must be revised in order to allow it to fit into the mainstream of scientific theory. As an example, Farrell (1981, p. 183) has drawn a parallel between psychoanalytic concepts and Lavoisier's concept of oxygen which had to be modified before combustion theory could be incorporated into the established body of scientific knowledge. So too might Freud's identification concept have to undergo changes before it will no longer languish outside the domain of empirical psychology.

In the second place, this account departs from Freud in that identification as a predictor of moral behaviour is proposed to be measurable through self-reports and to this extent is a cognitive process. But identification in this sense is not necessarily fully conscious. For it is entirely possible that a child may express a desire to be like a parent but at the same time be at a loss to explain why this is so. The cognitive and conscious aspects of identification can be distinguished. In Kagan's (1958, p. 298) terminology, identification is regarded as a cognitive response to command a goal state. But the content of the response may not be wholly conscious and fully verbalized.

This account departs as well from the traditional cognitive-developmental emphasis on cognitive development as a determinant of moral behaviour and the social learning emphasis on reinforcement and imitation. Though it does agree with arguments made by Ryle (1949) and Bem (1972) that self-knowledge is indirectly obtained from inferences based on one's own attitudes and behaviours in past circumstances, the indirect nature of such knowledge does not necessarily amount to inaccurate perceptions of oneself. Indeed, as Prior (1980, p. 212) has maintained, 'self-observers have a vast quantity of personal information available to them that outside observers could never practically obtain; this difference favours the accuracy of self-inference'.

Historically, the social-cognitive identification position is consistent with that taken originally by Baldwin (1896, 1906) and one which is undergoing a contemporary revival (Broughton 1981; J. Russell 1978). For Baldwin, children first have a projective sense of self in which the affective component of motivation predominates. They accommodate their behaviour to an ideal self as exemplified in the behaviour of others whom they perceive as good. Later these strivings to identify with parents' rules and standards for behaviour becomes more reflective in children's consciousness of the bases underlying their adulation of others. In this type of account, the concept of egocentric developmental stages is not accurate (Fine 1981, p. 32). The young child's sex-typed behaviour develops only *after* a definition of self with respect to significant and powerful others has been achieved; and a conception of 'self-in-relation-to-others is central to self-definition' (Lyons 1983, p. 141). Typically, the most important others are the child's parents.

Suppose it could be assumed that children are able to convey accurately their desires to be like their parents. In that event, the strength of identification might be measured by simply asking children questions such as 'Who do you want to be like when you grow up?' Children who maintain strongly that they would like to be similar to their parents could then be presumed to have a high degree of identification. The extent to which motivations and behaviour can be consciously and accurately verbalized by adults, let alone children, is once more a matter of continuing controversy (Nisbett and

Wilson 1977). Individuals, however, do demonstrate a considerable measure of consciousness about their own behavioural states. This awareness does not appear to require a sophisticated level of cognition (Kraut and Lewis 1982; White 1980).

Children's abilities to verbalize their motivations and behaviour accurately are largely unknown. But those who want to be like their parents may be more conscious of their wanting to identify than those who do not. Consequently, children's answers to questions seeking to establish the extent of their identifications may be one reasonable measure. Yet not all behaviours can be assumed to be mediated by identification since, at least, the parent will not be emulated in situations which demand sophisticated cognitive skills beyond those available to the child.

Most middle-class children, for example, have parents who maintain that they should follow school rules. Children who identify with their parents should internalize such rules, assuming that these are not beyond their level of cognitive development. In a study by Hoffman (1971), the participants were 13-year-old seventh graders from middle-class and lower-class homes in the Detroit area. As an 'identification index', the children were asked three questions: (a) 'Which person do you admire or look up to the most?' (b) 'Which person do you want to be like when you grow up?' and (c) 'Which person do you take after mostly?' Separate identification scores for mothers and fathers were obtained by adding the number of responses mentioning the mother and father respectively. Measures of rule conformity came from teacher's ratings of the extent to which the child usually follows or breaks the rules. Other measures included ones designed to assess guilt, confessions, and acceptance of blame. Data on guilt were collected by presenting children with the beginning of a story in which a child character has covertly transgressed (for example, a child cheats in a swimming race and wins). In completing the stories, subjects' reactions would be labelled as demonstrating guilt if these indicated self-criticism rather than a concern with external detection. Data on confession were gathered from mothers' responses to the interview question, 'When (name of child) has done something that he knows you would not approve of, and you haven't found out about it yet, how often does he come and tell you about it without your asking?' Teachers' reports of how the child reacts when 'caught doing something wrong' formed the basis for the index of blame acceptance.

Mother identification was significantly associated with rule conformity in middle-class boys and father identification was associated with rule conformity in both middle-class boys and girls. There were no significant associations in lower-class children, and no relationship between identification and guilt or blame acceptance in either social class groups. These results are not easy to interpret but Hoffman's tentative conclusion was that identification is not an 'all-pervasive process'; it contributes to children's rule-following behaviour though not that behaviour which occurs in the absence of authority. The identification process is seen to proceed most effectively between middle-class boys and their fathers since it is the middle-class father who, by acting emphatically toward the same-sex child, facilitates his identification.

There are several points to be noted about the Hoffman study. First, the measures of guilt, confession, and acceptance of blame are of questionable validity. There is no established association between actual behaviour and story-completion measures of guilt and the relation between guilt and behaviour is liable to be extremely complex (Karniol 1982). The story content itself varies enormously from a story for which the child may have a real-life acquaintance (winning a race by cheating) to one in which this acquaintance is usually lacking (contributing to the death of a younger child through negligence). The confession measures were based on teachers' reports of how children react to an authority figure following the discovery of a transgression and may not be indicative of a spontaneous, freely volunteered confession. The latter, based on parental reports, may be particularly unreliable and affected by a desire to give socially acceptable responses (Danziger 1971).

A second point is that children's actual behaviour may not be accurately reflected in the ratings of teachers (Babad, Inbar, and Rosenthal 1982; Bolstad and Johnson 1977). Rules may vary from teacher to teacher in content, extent of application, and enforcement and this variability enters into teacher ratings.

Third, as Hoffman mentions, these techniques may have been inadequate to investigate the cognitive prerequisites of much which would presumably be the outcome of identification. For example, it is possible that there are children who want to adopt the adult's behavioural rules and standards but do not actually do so because they are not yet able to understand the rules. Moreover, identification may be a more pervasive process at ages other than at the onset of adolescence (Mussen *et al.* 1970, p. 170).

Identification and rule-guided behaviour in the absence of external surveillance: a longitudinal study

In a previous study with regard to these issues (Siegal and Francis 1982), the subjects were 18 grade 1 children (14 girls and 4 boys) aged 5 and 6 years. Their rule-guided behaviour was observed in a naturalistic classroom situation. The children were given Hoffman's measure of identification and observed by a concealed videotape camera to determine the extent to which they abided by the rule not to disturb others during naptime or 'relaxation time'. When adult surveillance was withdrawn, and the teacher was absent from the classroom, a lack of self-reported mother identification accounted for a significant 34 per cent of the variance in reactions to others' rule-violating behaviour.

This initial study was limited in that it used a small, predominantly female sample and did not provide information as to whether identification is a behavioural antecedent. For this reason, a 3-year longitudinal study was devised (Siegal 1984*b*).

As Mussen *et al.* (1970) incisively noted, rule-following behaviour is sex-typed. Girls who have positive relations with their parents, particularly their mothers, will be more likely to adhere to rules than will boys. Those boys who are adequately sex-typed with their father will often display masculine behaviours in flaunting the rules. So in the absence of external surveillance, it was predicted that early mother identification should be related to later 'internalized', rule-guided behaviour, particularly for girls. Father identification, if at all associated with behaviour, should be related to rule-violations, particularly on the part of boys.

According to the cognitive-developmental approach, cognitive-developmental changes in conceptions of moral rules and social sex roles, assumed here to be congruent with behaviour which is sex-typed, should be 'causative forces' in the formation of parental identification. Thus rule-violating behaviour should be an antecedent of later parental identification; that is, a boy who demonstrates an early understanding of a male sex role by flaunting rules in a masculine sex-typed fashion will perceive himself later to be similar to the father as indicated by father identification.

According to the social-cognitive formulation, however, identification should precede behaviour. Thus children's early desire to be like a parent should predict their later behaviour. In line with the thesis of Chodorow and Gilligan, this sequence should be particularly evident for girls.

During the initial 2 years of the longitudinal study, the subjects were 67 children from two-parent families (37 boys and 30 girls). Their ages at the time of the first testing in grade 1 ranged from 5 years to 6 years 4 months (mean = 5 years 8 months). The children attended schools located in middle-class districts. They were distributed over four grade 1 classrooms, two of which were located in two different schools and the other two in a third school. By grade 3, the numbers had dropped to 34 boys and 26 girls. The children were lost to the study largely because their families had moved out of the school area.

The situation in grade 1 again involved napping periods which customarily form part of the children's day and are held soon after lunch each afternoon. Any deviation from a motionless state of napping could be scored as violating the rule not to engage in disturbing others during relaxation. This rule had been shown in the previous study to be regarded by children as generalized, collective, and moral according to the criteria of Nucci and Turiel (1978) which are discussed in Chapter 4 of this volume. The children's behaviour was videotaped by a concealed camera on six occasions. Each session took place in the regular time after lunch when the teacher announced, 'Time for your nap now, children'. She continued, as was usual, in reciting this rhyme:

> Quiet I shall sit
> Moving not a bit,
> Feet I shall rest,
> Head on my desk,
> Eyelids downward creep,
> Soon I'll be asleep.

Then she said, 'Remember the rule: it's not fair to disturb the other children during relaxation because they need their rest'.

After two minutes the session entered its second phase. The teacher told the children that she had to go out for a while and that they should remember the rule about remaining quiet and not disturbing others. When two further minutes elapsed, she reappeared in the room for the third phase of the session and told the subjects to keep napping. The period ended six minutes after it had begun.

Each child was also given measures of cognitive development (Goldschmidt and Bentler 1968) as well as the parental identification items used by Hoffman (1971). The children were asked to say whom they admire (or look up to or think the most of), whom they would want to be like as a grown-up, and whom they take after most.

Finally, since rule-violations may be related to peer group experience, each child was asked to state which classmates he or she would prefer to play with during freetime.

The procedure was repeated at yearly intervals when the children were in grades 2 and 3. Since the napping situation had become inappropriate now that the children were older, the major change was that their behaviour was covertly videotaped in the library. The children were seated at a desk reading a book which they themselves had chosen before silent reading period. The rule to be observed, as explained by the teacher at the start of the period, was to be quiet and not disturb others during reading time, in order so that they might learn.

Again the teacher was in the classroom for two minutes, then left for two minutes, and finally returned for the remaining two minutes. All the children had a different teacher in grade 2 and grade 3, and a different experimenter administered the tests. The grade 3 testing session was extended to include administration of a reading comprehension test (Elkins and Andrews 1974).

For each of the three phases in the sessions (adult present, adult absent, adult returns), the children's behaviour was scored for rule-violations in two categories: self-initiated rule violations directed toward disturbing others and rule-violations as reactions elicited from others' provocations. Talking, tossing and turning, and touching others were among the behaviours scored as rule-violations.

As would be expected, boys identified with their fathers more than with their mothers (mean scores = 0.54 and 0.19 respectively, SDs = 0.72 and 0.40). By contrast, girls identified with mothers more than fathers (mean scores = 0.60 and 0.21, SDs = 0.68 and 0.40).

Since mean numbers of rule-violations differed significantly across classes and observation years, and sex differences in both initiations and reactions emerged in grade 2, rule-violations of the boys and girls within each class on each of the six behavioural measures were transformed into z-scores. These were then combined together and factor-analysed. The analyses yielded a general factor accounting for over 50 per cent of the rule-violations for the boys and girls in grades 1 and 2. Since grade 3 girls committed very few rule-violations, only the boys' violations were transformed and factor-analysed in grade 3.

As shown in Table 2.1, consistent with the account derived from the cognitive-developmental model, boys' father identification in grade 3 was correlated positively with violations in grade 2 ($r = 0.30$, $p < 0.05$) while mother identification was correlated negatively

Table 2.1 Correlations between violation factor scores and mother and father identification, cognitive development, peer group popularity, reading, and birth order

		Boys				Girls		
		Grade 1	Grade 2	Grade 3	Autocorrelations	Grade 1	Grade 2	Autocorrelations
Mother identification	(1)	−0.18	−0.01	−0.06		−0.10	−0.34*	0.13
	(2)	−0.03	−0.34*	−0.03	0.00	0.13	0.13	0.39*
	(3)	0.07	−0.09	−0.16	−0.09	0.16	0.31	
Father identification	(1)	−0.07	0.10	−0.11		−0.08	0.08	−0.01
	(2)	0.19	0.04	−0.16	0.24	−0.06	−0.43**	0.02
	(3)	0.03	0.30*	0.15	0.32	0.06	0.43*	
Cognitive development	(1)	0.04	−0.21	−0.21		0.08	0.26	0.59**
Cognitive development	(2)	0.14	−0.11	−0.38*	0.33*	−0.20	0.05	0.14
Cognitive development	(3)	−0.04	−0.10	−0.20	0.47**	0.25	−0.02	
Peers	(1)	−0.04	0.11	−0.02		0.14	0.18	0.48**
Peers	(2)	0.13	0.14	0.09	0.32*	−0.12	0.26	0.62**
Peers	(3)	0.02	0.06	−0.04	0.48**	0.08	0.23	
Reading		−0.30	0.09	−0.41*		−0.10	−0.29	
Birth order		0.36*	0.23	0.03		−0.32	−0.24	
Autocorrelations			0.14	0.42**			0.30	

*p<0.05   **p<0.01

Autocorrelations are with scores in the previous year of testing.

For boys in grades 1 and 2 n=37; in grade 3, n=34.

For girls in grades 1 and 2, n=30; in grade 3, n=26. Correlations significant using one-tailed tests are underlined.

$(r = -0.34, p < 0.05)$. Grade 1 violations were correlated positively with birth order $(r = 0.36, p < 0.05)$, and there were negative correlations between grade 3 violations on the one hand and both cognitive development (grade 2) and reading on the other $(rs = -0.38, \text{ and } -0.41, ps < 0.05 \text{ and } 0.02 \text{ respectively})$. The correlation coefficient between factor scores at grades 1 and 2 was a non-significant 0.14; between scores at grades 2 and 3, it rose to 0.42 $(p < 0.01)$.

Thus for boys, identification with the same-sex parent follows masculine rule-flouting behaviour. For girls, a very different picture emerges.

In accordance with the position of Chodorow and Gilligan, mother identification in grade 1 preceded a lack of violations in grade 2 $(r = -0.34, p < 0.05)$. Grade 2 violations also were correlated negatively with father identification in grade 2 $(r = -0.43, p < 0.01)$. Father identification in grade 3, however, was positively correlated with grade 2 violations $(r = 0.43, p < 0.05)$ which is parallel to the boys' data. But contrary to the results for boys, violations in grade 1 were correlated negatively with birth order $(r = -0.32, p < 0.05)$. The correlation coefficient between the factor scores for the two grades was 0.30 $(p < 0.05)$.

The predicted association between identification and behaviour was strongest in the absence of external authority. Reactions in the absent phase for grade 2 girls were negatively correlated with their mother identification in grade 1, $r = -0.49, p < 0.01)$. Reactions also were negatively related to father identification in grade 2 $(r = -0.43, p < 0.02)$ and reading $(r = -0.40, p < 0.05)$, two measures which were correlated together $(r = 0.40, p < 0.05)$. Father identification in grade 1 was associated positively with grade 2 initiations (returns phase, $r = 0.39, p < 0.05)$. In sharp opposition to the positive correlations between boys' rule-violations and birth order, girls' birth order was correlated negatively with initiation in grade 1 (present phase, $r = -0.43, p < 0.01)$ and initiations in grade 2 (returns phase, $r = -0.37, p < 0.05)$. Firstborn girls were more likely to initiate violations than those born later. The correlation between mother identification scores for grades 1 and 2 was a non-significant 0.13, and that between scores for grades 2 and 3 was 0.39 $(p < 0.05)$. All other significant results for girls involved father identification in grade 3 which correlated positively with violations in the second grade (initiations, present phase, $r = 0.39, p < 0.05$; reactions, returns phase, $r = 0.46, p < 0.01)$.

For boys, initiations in the absent phase of grade 2 were negatively associated with mother identification in grade 2 $(r = -0.38, p < 0.05)$

and positively with father identification in grade 3 ($r=0.43$, $p<0.01$). In general, boys' reading and cognitive development in both grades 2 and 3 were correlated negatively with grade 3 violations. For cognitive development in grade 2, there was a significant relationship involving initiations in the present and absent phases of grade 3 ($rs=-0.53$ and -0.41, $ps<0.01$ and 0.02 respectively) as well as reactions in the absent phase ($r=-0.34$, $p<0.05$). Reactions also correlated with reading scores ($r=-0.45$, $p<0.01$).

Birth-order effects emerged once more in grade 3. Later-born boys were less likely to identify with their fathers ($r=0.44$, $p<0.01$) and were more likely to be chosen by their peers on the measure of popularity ($r=0.60$, $p<0.01$).

Self-definition in the context of significant other persons

Bearing in mind that the results are based on a small sample and that the number of significant correlations is relatively few, there is support for the social-cognitive account in the girls' case. Identification with the mother in grade 1 was negatively related to grade 2 violations. The mother preceded the father as a predictor of girls' ability to resist others' misconduct. Yet the father, as emulated in grade 3, was positively associated with rule-violations in grade 2. The existence of this sequence is consistent with the cognitive-developmental account that identification is preceded by sex-typing. Girls who flout rules would appear to be inappropriately sex-typed and they may later opt to emulate the father. Rule-violations when an adult authority is present would seem to reflect a fearlessness which is particularly masculine for girls.

As Kohlberg (1966, p. 142) has maintained, for boys, 'moral niceness' tends to be stereotyped as a feminine speciality, and as a result there is a certain conflict between masculine sex-typing and morality, between being a 'real boy' and 'being good'. In the present study, boys' initiations in grade 2 when the adult was absent were correlated negatively with mother identification in grade 2 and positively with father identification in grade 3 providing clear evidence for Kohlberg's position. In keeping with this account, compared to girls, a developmental delay occurs in the relationship between sex-typed behaviour and boys' identification with the same-sex parent.

If this relationship were mediated by cognitive development it would bear a close affinity to Kohlberg's statement that father identification is a byproduct of cognitive-developmental changes in sex-role identity which undermines the boys' early affectional tie with the mother. There were no significant simultaneous correlations, however, between cognitive development and either identification or behaviour and no significant correlation across time-lags between cognitive development in grades 1 or 2 and either type of measure in grades 2 or 3.

Though, as Kohlberg (1969) notes, fathers' masculinity may be uncorrelated with son's masculine behaviour, it does not follow that identification is a mere byproduct of changes in sex-roles for both boys and girls. The more parsimonious interpretation is that the sequence of identification in boys reflects a lack of father participation in childcare relative to the mother and female teachers (Block 1983, p. 1347; Chodorow 1978). Consequently, the young boy generally does not develop the same close intimate relationship with his father that the girl has with her mother. Even in so-called non-traditional families, the father's role as primary caretaker of pre-schoolers appears to diminish considerably with time with many families reverting back to a traditional lifestyle (G. Russell 1982). Ordinarily the boy is set adrift to search for the appropriate role model. His self-definition in terms of the attributes of his father is a product rather than an antecedent of his sex-typed behaviour. Such a mechanism may not be restricted to boys for girls at the same time in grade 3 also show evidence of identifying with their fathers after they engage in rule-violations. The contemporary father may often not provide the impetus which the young boy requires to display a concern for others and refrain from rule-violations. Should the boy perceive the father to have specific prosocial qualities such as a sense of empathy or 'fairness', he may be more willing to resist the temptation to misbehave (Francis and Siegal, 1984; see also Chapters 6 and 8 of this volume). Compared to the relationship between mothers and daughters, an intimate father–son relationship may not occur until late childhood or adolescence—if at all.

In the absence of adult authority, the associations between identification and behaviour generally involved reactions for girls and initiations for boys. Beyond illustrating the need to distinguish between categories of rule-violating behaviour, the pattern of results is indicative of the different orientations taken by boys and girls toward rules. Rule-violating in boys is a manifestation of their autonomy and separateness. Initiations reflect this masculine sex-typed orientation and lead to father identification. For girls, rule-violating is more a matter of selflessly joining in a relationship with others. Reactions are a clear manifestation of a feminine sex-typed orientation and are preceded by the lack of a close relationship with the mother. In this study, sex of subject did not significantly differentiate rule-violations in grade 1; initiations clearly predominated for both sexes. By contrast, in the absent phase of grade 2, girls' violations were almost evenly divided in frequency between initiations and reactions (48.8 *vs.* 51.2 per cent); for boys, initiations predominated over reactions (58.7 *vs.* 41.3 per cent). Similar sex differences have been found in adults' rule-violating behaviour (Osman 1982). The sex-related dichotomy between initiations and reactions neatly fits the theses of Chodorow and Gilligan.

Relationships involving gender and birth order have been found previously. In a study by Laosa and Brophy (1972) using children aged 5 and 6 years, firstborn boys and later-born girls were observed to prefer to play alone significantly more than their same-sex peers. The unexpected pattern of relations between initiations and birth order in the present study are similar with firstborn boys and later-born girls showing fewer violations as initiations in the return phase of grade 1 and the present phase of grade 2 respectively. Firstborn boys may be more socialized to achieve at school and have no older siblings to present a sex-typed model of behaviour. Thus they deviate less than later-borns. By contrast, firstborn girls are expected to be more independent than later-borns and have no older siblings to present a sex-typed model of behaviour.

Laosa and Brophy also found that firstborn boys are more likely to say that their fathers are the smartest, consistent with their greater father identification as indicated in the present study. Firstborn grade 2 boys were in addition less likely to initiate violations when an adult is present, consistent with the results of a recent observational study by Hinde *et al.* (1983) who observed firstborns to be more adult-oriented in their social interactions than are later-borns. Finally, the correlation between birth order and peer-group popularity adds to the volume of literature which has found both early- and later-borns to be more popular (see Snow, Jacklin, and Maccoby 1981).

Overall, these results suggest that children's self-definition as a form of identification can play a role in the process of internalization and moral development, particularly as an antecedent of girls' rule-guided behaviour observed naturalistically in a commonly occurring school situation. Should a longer measure of identification be developed, the correlations should either remain the same or increase. A lack of stability in the measures over 1 year allows for the possibility of a type II error rather than a type I error; instead of uncovering false relationships, those which do exist will not be found (Johnson and Bolstad 1973; Yarrow and Waxler 1979). Predictability might be enhanced by combining a larger number of identification items using the principle of aggregation (Epstein 1980). Caution, however, should be exercised with regard to the matter of causal connections. Correlational data alone does not demonstrate that a cause produces an effect but provides an incentive for experimental manipulations in further research. Baumrind (1983*b*) treats in detail an example of the specious inferences that can be drawn when correlations are wrongly assumed to demonstrate a causal relationship.

The low temporal stability of the identification scores is consistent with the notion that variables which are important at one point in development are irrelevant at other points. While identification 'attitudes' have been viewed as 'age-specific reactions to developmental tasks' (Kohlberg 1966, p. 126), it is at least equally plausible that self-definition changes over time, particularly during the early school years. The mix of ingredients which make up a child's self-definition become the basis for later behaviour. By the time that behaviour is shown, the child's self-definition has changed and shows no significant synchronous relation with current behaviour. In the girls' case, the mother may have an impact in grade 1 which does not appear until grade 2. At this time, even the weak negative correlation in grade 1 between reactions and identification has now disappeared owing to the impact of new school experiences and significant non-parental figures which enter into the girl's self-definition. When considering the lack of significant synchronous correlations, it should be kept in mind that the children were asked questions which pertain to their future behaviour as adults.

Much of the place of cognitive development may be seen in terms of the child's consciousness of what mothers and fathers are perceived to offer the young child as a guide for behaviour. Cognitive development measured in terms of logical abilities, an ability to take the role of the other, or hypothetical moral dilemmas, may be significantly associated with certain aspects of rule-guided behaviour. But such measures do not necessarily provide behavioural antecedents when compared with the predictive power of identificatory measure of self-definition which focus on a hot cognition having a high affective importance to the person.

Identification is not a process which once merited attention as a 'flavour of the month'. It provides an illustration of the treasures contained within the history of psychology (Henle 1976). In the construction of a comprehensive theory of socialization, it is not a sideshow to rule-guided behaviour but an integral feature. It is a construct relevant to the moral and social development which involves a concern for others' welfare.

3

Intellectual performance in context

Borrowing from Maehr's (1974, p. 4) definition, achievement consists of measurable changes in behaviour that can be attributed to an individual as a causal agent, can be evaluated in terms of a standard of excellence, and typically involves some uncertainty as to the outcome of an individual's performance. The lion's share of the research on achievement has resolved around intellectual performance as shown on school reports of grades and standardized tests of mathematical and verbal ability. Whether children's achievement is determined primarily by their past performance or by their perceptions of parents' expectations has been the source of much controversy.

Attributions for past performance

The notion that individuals' reasoning about their past behaviour contributes to their self-perceptions of the ability and effort required in achievement situations gained hold with the writings of Fritz Heider. The key aspects of Heider's position are contained in his 1958 book *The psychology of interpersonal relations* which was mainly concerned with issues in adult social psychology. One central proposition is that persons perceive behaviour as being caused and as 'naive scientists' attempt to infer causes from the effects of specific, fixed behaviours. Causal inferences are associated with general psychological dispositions. These inferences come from two sources: (1) individuals' knowledge of personal characteristics such as ability and effort; and (2) external or environmental forces such as task difficulty. We are said to attribute our behaviour to causes in an attempt to find meaning and structure in our social interactions. Since young children may not have as accurate and as comprehensive a knowledge of their past performances as do adults, causal attributions based on past performances may not be as relevant to children's general psychological dispositions as to adults.

Nevertheless, Heider's ideas have inspired a great amount of research involving children as well as adults. Two premises which have underscored attention to causal attributions are that attributions are related to behaviour, and that changes in attributions should lead to changes in behaviour. Over the past 15 years, much work has been devoted to documenting the development of causal attributions.

In a pioneering series of experiments, Weiner and Kukla (1970) have provided evidence that individuals who are highly motivated to achieve are likely to approach achievement-related activities because they ascribe success to their own effort and ability rather than to luck or to the simplicity of the task. Failure is interpreted as due to a lack of effort rather than to a lack of ability or to the difficulty of the task.

On this basis, groups of children other than white, middle-class boys have been hypothesized to perceive their behaviour as caused by environmental or external factors over which they have little control. Friend and Neale (1972), for example, gave 125 fifth-graders a brief reading test. Some were told 'You did much better than most boys and girls of your grade'; a second group were told 'You did much worse than most boys and girls of your grade'; and a third were given no feedback. Then all the children were asked to evaluate the importance of ability, effort, task difficulty, and luck in relation to their performance. There were no sex or social class differences, but white children judged that ability and effort were relatively more important for their performance than task difficulty and luck, while the reverse was true for black children. The suggestion is that black children perform more poorly in school than white children because they attribute their success and failure to factors over which they have little control. Effort and ability are comparatively unimportant.

A number of other studies have dealt specifically with sex differences in attributions for achievement. Perhaps the most notable are two experiments reported in an article by Dweck *et al.* (1978). In the first, the subjects were fourth and fifth-graders attending a predominantly white, lower-class state school in the Champaign, Illinois, area. Observations were carried out in the children's five classrooms over a period of 5 weeks for 2 full days a week. Instances of evaluative feedback from teachers to students were coded into whether these were relevant to the task in referring to the competence of the child's performance or irrelevant, referring to neatness, rules of form, or quality of speech. In absolute terms, boys received more than three times the amount of negative feedback and a higher frequency of relevant intellectual criticism than did girls. As a percentage of total negative feedback for each sex, however, girls received more criticism relating to the intellectual inadequacy of their work and fewer irrelevant evaluations for neatness or rules of form.

According to Dweck *et al.* (1978) intellectual inadequacy in girls is fostered by their receiving a greater proportion of evaluations relevant to the competence of their performance. Having received intellectual criticism, they attribute failure to a lack of ability. By contrast, a high proportion of criticism directed at boys is irrelevant and non-intellectual, and thus boys attribute failure to a lack of effort. In an experimental follow-up study, the relevance of criticism for failure in children's attempts at solving anagrams (a non-school material) was manipulated. The results were interpreted to support the contention that the different types of evaluations which boys and girls receive at school contribute to differences in their motivation to achieve.

The studies of Dweck *et al.* were guided by the attributional approach, one which is described most prominently in the writings of Weiner (1980). The past performances of the child produce specific information about success and failure which lead to causal inferences. The most salient of these are ability and effort. These inferences mediate children's motivation to achieve. The attributional model is shown in Fig. 3.1. Weiner (p. 369) illustrates this

Fig. 3.1. The attributional model of Weiner (1980, p. 388).

process by providing what he regards as 'cognition-emotion' scenario which is something like that experienced by the typical student on receiving the results of examinations:

(a) 'I just received a "D" in the exam. That is a very low grade' (this generates feelings of being frustrated and upset). 'I received this grade because I just am not smart enough' (followed by feelings of incompetence and lack of confidence). 'There really is something lacking in me, and it is permanent' (followed by low self-esteem or lack of worth and hopelessness).

(b) 'I just received an "A" in the exam. That is a very high grade' (generating happiness and satisfaction). 'I received this grade because I worked very hard during the entire school year' (producing contentment and relaxation). 'I really do have some positive qualities, and will continue to have them in the future' (followed by high self-esteem and feelings of self-worth, as well as optimism for the future).

The findings of Dweck *et al.* (1978), however, have not been generally supported in a study by Parsons, Adler, and Kaczala (1982). While this attempt at replication was not strictly comparable in that maths alone was used as a subject matter and the students were of a higher social class, many other studies have also yielded no sizeable sex differences. These have often used the Intellectual Achievement Responsibility Scale (Crandall, Katkovsky, and Crandall 1965) in which children are presented with forced choice alternatives as attributions for performance in achievement situations, each of which contrasts an internal cause (such as 'trying hard') against an external cause (such as the ease of the task or the assistance of others). Those differences that do emerge actually provide support for the conclusions of Dweck *et al.* (1978) in reverse: that girls cite effort as the cause of their performance more than do boys (Cooper, Burger, and Good 1981). The degree to which causal attributions contribute to sex differences in achievement motivation, should such differences prove to be authentic, remains uncertain. Young children, in particular, may simply not have had enough experience to formulate any sort of stable attributions to guide their efforts at achievement. They may be oblivious to comparisons of how well they perform relative to others and, if anything, may perceive a lack of ability as an unstable factor subject to fluctuations (Ruble *et al.* 1980).

Other more recent studies have examined the relation between children's knowledge of a teacher's affective reactions toward a failing student, such as anger, pity, guilt, surprise, and sadness, and their causal inferences (Weiner *et al.* 1982). Anger is seen by children to be associated with lack of effort on the part of the student and pity with a lack of ability. It is suggested that the teacher's expressed pity could lead to students' attributing their failings to a lack of ability, resulting in poor achievement motivation. No sex differences were evident here either.

The current state of affairs has been sized up neatly by Sohn (1982). Out of 28 studies dealing with sex differences in attributions of one's performance to ability, males made more ability attributions than females in six, and females more than males in seven. There were no sex differences in the remainder of the studies. Commenting on the lack of reliability in these effects, Sohn (1982, pp. 355–6) concludes:

. . . the failure to find evidence of consequential relationships between sex and attribution behaviour does not mean that such relationships do not or cannot be found to exist. It does mean that present claims of the general importance of these relationships do not have empirical support. It also means that more specific claims or intimations of the deleterious nature of female (in contrast to male) self-attributions are not warranted at the present time.

If girls can be shown to have a lower motivation to achieve, this may be more closely tied to their perceptions of parental expectations than to their past performances in school. Clearly, parents have different expectations for girls and boys. Success for boys may be attributed to high ability and girls' success put down to hard work. For example, daughters may not be expected to be as good at mathematics as are sons and their concepts of their mathematical ability may reflect these expectations.

In the extensive questionnaire study of 22 fifth to eleventh-grade classrooms in Ann Arbor, Michigan, conducted by Parsons, Adler and Kaczala (1982), students and parents were asked to respond to items concerning their past, present, and future motivation to achieve at mathematics. The students rated the difficulty of their current and future mathematics courses, their current and future expectancies of performance, and the perception of effort involved in mathematics. They were also asked to rate perceptions of their parents' perceptions of ability and parents' expectations for performance. Similarly, parents themselves were questioned as to the difficulty, effort, and importance which they have attached to mathematics in the past and present. In addition, they were asked to indicate the importance and difficulty of mathematics which they perceive for their child together with their perception of the child's ability.

Analyses of these responses showed that the self-concepts and expectations of both boys and girls were more directly related to their parents' attitudes about their abilities than to their own past performances. Perceptions of the mothers' expectations yielded higher correlations than those of fathers', and parents of daughters had lower expectations than did parents of sons. However, sex differences in ability self-concept were slight, and there were no sex differences in actual school marks. Moreover, prior to the twelfth grade, there were no significant differences in enrolment in maths courses (Eccles 1983, p. 115; Eccles, Adler, and Meece 1984).

The results of the study by Parsons, Adler and Kaczala suggest that childrens' past performance does not owe as much to motivation as to parental expectations for the future. Neither boys nor girls believe their past performance actually affects their parents' expectations, and parents perceive both sons and daughters to have identical ability or 'achievement potential'. One representation of this

Fig. 3.2.   Achievement potential model.

model is shown in Fig. 3.2. Assuming high parental expectations, an alternative scenario can be written to fit the model:

(a)   'I just received a "D" in the exam. That is a very low grade' (this generates feelings of fear and guilt with the knowledge that one's parents have been let down). 'I received this grade not because I haven't the brains but because I didn't study hard enough and the exam was hard this time. I'll tell my parents that I'll try harder next time' (accompanied by feelings that parental expectations will not be altered and optimism for the future).
(b)   'I just received an "A" in the exam. That is a very good grade. I can't wait to tell my parents' (this generates feelings of pride and happiness). 'Consistent with their expectations I received this grade because I knew the material on the exam and spent a lot of time studying' (accompanied by feelings that parental expectations will not be altered accompanied by high self-esteem, self-worth, and optimism for the future).

In both cases, parental expectations are perceived by children to be stable and not subject to variations on the basis of performance. This may reflect an 'ego-defensive bias' in attributions in which children take more credit for their successes and less for their failures than would be allowed by observers of their performance. Parents as observers may be more likely than are children themselves to revise their expectations on a performance basis, and for boys in particular. Should girls do poorly on a mathematics test, for example, parents may not take this evidence as seriously as for boys. Mathematics is regarded by both mothers and fathers as more important for boys than for girls. Thus if girls do have less motivation to achieve in mathematics, it may be because they share these perceptions that a knowledge of mathematics is irrelevant to their futures. Support for the position that 'subjective task value' mediates academic achievement plans in general and sex differences in general comes from a follow-up study by Eccles (Parsons), Adler, and Meece (1984) based on the same sample as the original Parsons, Adler, and Kaczala (1982) study. While self-concept of ability for both sexes is linked to actual academic performance, perceptions of the value of a subject matter are not surprisingly an important influence on students' decisions to pursue the study of a subject. A special effort is needed to overcome these perceptions of irrelevancy just as a special motivation may be needed by all children to study a subject such as Sanskrit, or Old English, which may not be foreseen by parents to be relevant to their children's futures. According to Stein and Bailey (1973, pp. 363–4), though girls generally do better than boys in high school, ultimately at the university level 'reduced achievement efforts occur for many young women partly because there is pressure to adhere to feminine role definitions and because females internalize the low expectations of the culture for their continued achievement'.

Sex and past performance may colour parents' expectations of their children's achievement, but the role played by the characteristics of the child in forming expectations should be viewed in context. 'Microsystem' variables which are located immediately within the parent–child relationship can be considered together with other variables embedded within the mesosystem and exosystem. Parents' expectations of the importance of actual achievement could be altered by a host of factors unrelated to their sons' and daughters' past performance at school. These include the availability of places for girls in courses which have been traditionally male-dominated, the acceptance of women into traditionally male-dominated occupations, and the perceived desirability of maternal employment and the two-income family. Parents may hold sex-typed beliefs on their child's achievement potential, not because they regard sons as having higher ability than daughters, but because daughters' abilities do not assume the same importance in the economic world. Needless to say, parental expectations for children of both sexes can vary with changes in socioeconomic circumstances.

Girls may come to adopt parental expectations for their futures as their own, and girls' career plans are frequently vaguer than are boys'. In an extensive study of adolescents' career plans (Douvan and Adelson 1966), girls reported fewer decisive goals to accomplish as adults than did boys. The desire to pursue a career was claimed by most. But far from providing a realistic picture, often these aspirations were expressed on a fantasy level such as becoming a famous actress. Implications for women's self-confidence arise from an unclear orientation for achievement. Contrary to the prevalent assumption, women's self-reported confidence in achievement situations is not generally lower than that of men; it is usually apparent only when the extent to which successful performance on a task is vague and unclear, or where the nature of the task is a masculine one or subject to evaluation from others (Lenney 1977; Lenney and Gold 1982).

Overall, parental expectations may form the single most important source of influence on children's achievement motivation, even when compared to the influence wielded by peers. In a review of the achievement ambitions of adolescents, Spenner and Featherman (1978, p. 392) conclude that 'The encouragement of one's parents and the plans of one's peers appear to shape ambitions more directly and with greater impact than any other source. Their effects are stronger than the direct influence of one's scholastic attitude or previous academic achievement, and much stronger than any direct influence from one's social origins per se.'

Guided by these conclusions, Davies and Kandel (1981) sought to compare the strengths of parental and peer influences in an extensive survey of the educational plans of adolescents living in New York State. Whether measured by the subjects' perceptions of their parents' and peers' educational expectations or the actual expectations as reported by parents and peers, parental influences were greater for adolescents at all ages. When compared to those of peers, parental influences grew stronger with age and were connected with boys' plans in particular. The higher correlation between parental influences and boys' plans may be due to a greater lack of achievement responsibility among boys, leaving a wider area for parental encouragement. Or it may be that educational plans and parental expectations simply show a wider variation for boys than for girls.

A number of studies have been consistent with the conclusion that parental encouragement exerts a more potent influence on educational plans than one's direct social origins. These have confirmed that actual academic achievement is more highly correlated with family characteristics such as 'home atmosphere' than with family income which in turn is correlated more highly with academic achievement than with parental occupation (K. R. White 1982).

Two questions, however, emerge from these findings for which as yet there are no completely satisfactory answers: (1) What is the direction of effect in the correlation between parental influence and children's achievement motivation and behaviour? (2) What is the nature of this influence?

Socialization and intellectual performance: the search for a causal connection

Do bright, achieving children affect parents' achievement expectations? Or is the reverse more likely? Do parental expectations create a motivation to achieve? Despite all the cross-sectional evidence, there is only one longitudinal study to date which has systematically addressed this issue. As Henderson (1981) points out, even this study which dealt with the intellectual performances of very young children has serious shortcomings.

Bradley, Caldwell, and Elardo (1979) used a cross-lagged panel analysis to investigate the relation between home environment and cognitive development. One of the main environmental measures was maternal involvement. Mothers and children with predominantly lower-class and lower-middle class were observed when the children were 6, 12, and 24 months. The degree to which the mother encouraged the child's intellectual challenges and social experiences was recorded. At these times each child was also administered the Bayley Scales of Infant Development as a measure of cognitive development.

There was some suggestion in the results that bright children at 6 months influenced maternal involvement at 12 months (rather than the reverse) and that maternal involvement at 12 months led to brighter children at 24 months (rather than the reverse). But the correlations were all below 0.33 and were dwarfed by the high correlations on the measures themselves between 6 and 12 months and between 12 and 24 months. With a larger sample of children clearer connections between achievement and expectations might have been found. In the case of adolescents' intellectual performance, the issue may eventually be illuminated by Eccles' ongoing longitudinal study at the University of Michigan.

Whether or not parents' expectations and behaviour are in any sense strongly dependent upon the child's early achievements, the quality of the home environment can be influential. In a study by Norman-Jackson (1982), 21 preschoolers in low-income black families living in New York City were observed in their homes and their verbal interactions tape-recorded. Fourteen children who had been the subjects of home observation at 24–42 months were evaluated for reading achievement in grades 1 or 2. Though successful readers did differ from unsuccessful ones in their preschool IQ, they had participated in more verbal interactions with their familes as preschoolers. Also, more encouragement and less discouragement accompanied their verbal initiations. Their parents were less likely to give responses such as 'go away', 'shut up', or 'don't bother me'. A number of similar studies are reviewed by Henderson (1981).

The Norman-Jackson study was limited in that it did not examine parental attributes such as reading preferences or intelligence. Especially literate parents may create an environment which fosters literate children, or it may be that children of literate parents would be literate regardless of variation in their verbal stimulation.

A widely acknowledged problem in interpreting such results is that environmental and genetic influences are confounded (Willerman 1979). The heredity–environment (nature–nurture) debate on sources of intelligence is a complex matter and beyond the scope of this chapter. But assuming that some significant variation in correlations between the intelligence of parents and children can be attributed to environmental sources (Mackenzie 1984; Rose *et al.* 1980), it makes sense to ask in what way do children's perceptions of parental expectations motivate achievement.

Inspired by Robert White's (1959) classic paper, much research has centred on the prospect of providing home and school environments which foster children's motivation toward competence, a motivation which is satisfied by feelings of 'efficacy'. The object is to arrange learning environments in order to have children perceive adults' expectations that independent attempts at the mastery of a subject matter will lead to successful performance.

With regard to one of the child's earliest achievements, the development of vocabulary, the quality of time allotted to childcare can have an effect. Leibowitz (1977) found that both a mother's self-reported reading to the child and reading to herself correlated with preschoolers' vocabulary development on the Peabody Picture Vocabulary Test (PPVT). Moreover, there was a significant association between PPVT scores and the presence of labour-saving devices in the home. Families of similar income and education in the study had either colour televisions or dishwashers and dryers. The presence of the latter and the absence of the former appeared to release more time for the mother's involvement with the child. Parents' interest in verbal achievement as indicated by the presence of an encyclopaedia made an independent positive contribution to the children's scores.

Achievement in older children and adolescents, as well as preschoolers, has been explored using a variety of measures designed to measure the child's locus of control or perceived competence (Crandall, Katkovsky, and Crandall 1965; Harter 1981, 1982*b*; Mischel, Zeiss, and Zeiss 1974; Nowicki and Duke 1974, 1979). These measures are concerned with the child's sense of personal control over his or her accomplishments.

Control and parental expectations

The Intellectual Achievement Responsibility (IAR) scale developed by Crandall *et al.* pertains to children's perceived control over the outcome of school achievement situations in grade 3 and above, while the Mischel *et al.* scale is specifically geared for preschoolers. The Nowicki–Strickland Locus of Control Scale has versions for preschoolers, schoolchildren, and adults (Nowicki and Strickland 1973; Nowicki and Duke 1974, 1979). The preschool and primary version consists of 34 items. Three factors which emerge from a factor analysis of the responses of children aged 5–8 years have been labelled 'power *vs.* helplessness', 'persistence in dealing with parents', and 'luck'. Sample items corresponding to these factors were: 'Can you make others kids like you? Most of the time do you find it easy to get your own way at home? Are most kids just born good at running races?' Those with an internal locus of control respond 'Yes' to the first two questions and 'No' to the third. Versions of these scales discriminate between achieving and non-achieving 8 year old girls (Nowicki and Duke 1974), and between learning disabled and normal achieving 10-year-old boys (Fincham and Barling 1978).

Nowicki and Segal (1974) examined the correlates of locus of control. Their subjects were 162 white twelfth-graders from a lower-middle class family background living in a suburban area of a large city in the southeastern United States. The students were asked to complete a version of the Nowicki–Strickland scale three times: as for themselves, for their mothers, and for their fathers. They were also asked to fill out a rating scale of perceived parental attributes of nurturance on dimensions of affection, physical contact, security, and trust.

Correlations between children's locus of control and the perceived locus of control of their parents were significant (0.57 for boys, 0.36 for girls). As for studies in which the IAR scale had been used, boys were significantly more external than girls. Internal control was correlated only with mothers' affection (0.31). For girls, parental influence was considerably greater. All attributes except one (father's encouragement) were significantly related to self-reported internality. These correlations ranged from 0.32 to 0.58. For girls only, internality was associated with participation in extracurricular activities (0.37). The perceived internal control of fathers was correlated significantly with girls' achievement test scores on composition (0.35), reading (0.25), and mathematics (0.28). The explanation given by Nowicki and Segal is that girls with perceived internal fathers are expressing an incongruity between the 'accepted' female cultural role of passivity and conformity. In the longitudinal study described in the previous chapter (Siegal 1984*b*), there were correlations between girls' father identification and rule-violating behaviour incongruous with the female stereotype.

A follow-up study (Wichern and Nowicki 1976) using second and seventh-graders as subjects indicated that seventh-grade internals perceive their mothers to be more lax than did externals. Compared to mothers of externals, mothers of internals reported significantly earlier ages for independence training and allowing independence. It is suggested that self-reliance is fostered by internal mothers which 'serves to connect the child to internal perceptions'. Similar results have been found by Chandler *et al.* (1980).

None of these measures account for a tremendously impressive proportion of the variance in intellectual performance. Standardized test scores are predicted better than are school grades perhaps because grades are partly a reflection of teachers' subjective judgements of performance and are somewhat independent of children's perceived control (Findley and Cooper 1983). Further, questions about the reliability of such measures have been raised (see Kagan *et al.* 1982).

Harter (1978, 1981, 1982*b*) has asserted that White's notion of effectance motivation should not be regarded as a global or unitary construct. Rather, in order to enhance the predictability of children's school success, it is necessary to delineate the possible components of 'systems' of motivation. To this end, self-report scales of intrinsic motivation, for example, have been devised consisting of five subscale dimensions: challenge, curiosity, mastery, judgement, and criteria (Harter and Pike 1984). These measures are still in their infancy and their utility remains to be shown.

Expectations and attributions in context

In sum, the demonstrated associations between control and intellectual performance relate, albeit modestly, to children's perceptions of parental expectations and characteristics. A theory which leans heavily on causal inferences for past performance, such as a lack of effort or ability, without linking inferences to expectations, is likely to fall short of what is needed to provide a full account of children's achievement motivation and future intellectual performance. This sort of attribution approach may even do for this area what cognitive–developmental approaches have done for moral development: to cut behaviour off from its context in the social relations between parents and children. As Semin (1980, pp. 297–8) has written:

it is obvious that we do not construct social reality from scratch every morning when we get up; however, it is not clear in attribution theory *when* we make attributions and *when* we do *not*. If it were the case that we had to explain the causes of behaviour constantly the cognitive load would be intolerable, and we would have our man literally lost in thought. . . . Only when social reality has slipped temporarily through our fingers, do we need to invest some effort in constructing the reality. . . . Attribution theory's chief shortcoming . . . is its disregard for the social context of everyday existence, and this shortcoming is manifest in the model of man implicit in the theory.

In keeping with Semin's comments, Covington and Omelich (1979, 1984) have shown that adult intellectual performance may be mediated more by expectancies than by attributions for past outcomes. Deaux (1984) has provided an expectancy model of adult attributional processes in which cultural stereotypes dictate specific task expectations. Performance consistent with expectations is associated with attributions to stable and internal causes while performance inconsistent with expectations is associated with attributions to unstable causes. The complex task of reconciling attribution theory with an expectancy value approach is discussed in a collection of articles edited by Feather (1982).

With regard to children's performance, it can be said that prediction processes may be more directly important than attributional ones. Attributions consist of going from a concrete act of success or failure to a general disposition to achieve based on causal inferences. By contrast, prediction requires that the 'situation be put back into the equation' (Schneider, Hastorf, and Ellsworth 1979, p. 200). Future expectations provided by parents can reconcile situational performance to a general disposition. Ordinarily, children's attributions are directed outside themselves to the expectancies of others and they do not normally dwell upon their own causal attributions for past successes and failures. In this case, attributions and expectancies are influenced by subject matter. Mathematics, for example, may be seen as an intellectually demanding task which gives clear feedback on performance. Attributions for achievement in mathematics may be more influential in determining students' self-concepts of mathematical ability than are, for example, attributions for achievement in English literature for determining English ability self-concepts.

The evidence for causal connections in either the moral or intellectual sphere is flimsy. What is clear in either case is that self-processes are related to perceptions of significant others and particularly parents. Questions which cry out for investigation are: By what means does the child expect encouragement from parents to meet their expectations? Does the child have 'standards for parenthood' just as the parent has standards for the child's behaviour and, if so, how are these related to perceptions of control?

Parents, peers, and children's appraisals of others' behaviour

According to Lewis (1981), the child's behaviour may reflect internal perceptions of control and a willingness to obey rather than the degree to which parents themselves exercise control *per se*. Neither firm control nor punishment may be necessary to obtain the child's compliance and the exercise of parental control may often be superfluous to socialization.

Based on an attributional analysis that children's behavioural development is encouraged by internal perceptions, Lepper (1983) suggests that subtle childrearing methods be used to minimize the young child's perception of external constraint. By contrast, Baumrind (1983*a*) argues that control techniques must be salient and that external inducements for prosocial behaviour are more effective. To examine the relation between techniques and attributions, Dix and Grusec (1983) had parents and children make causal attributions for the helping behaviour of story characters. External attributions were offered when characters were ordered to help and the consequence of non-compliance was specified. Descriptions of characters' spontaneous modelling of helping behaviour and helping in response to parents' reasoning (such as 'I bet you'd like to help') produced internal attributions. Though this study did not examine children's evaluations of techniques perceived as likely to result in compliance, research on attributional processes can be integrated with work on children's understanding of maternal intervention and rule enforcement.

The Piagetian approach

For Piaget (1977*b*), the young child's perceptions of the social world are marked by egocentrism, an inability to consider different points of view simultaneously and understand the rationale behind rules designed to regulate behaviour. Appel (1977) hypothesized that egocentric children have an inadequate grasp of the psychological variable of intentionality and would not be likely to understand the basis for a mother's strictness. It was predicted that young ego-centric children do not have a conception of good maternal care and would be likely to prefer a permissive mother who allows mis-behaviour to a mother who intervenes. By contrast, older non-egocentric children have a greater understanding of the rationale be-hind enforcing rules aimed to prevent misbehaviour. Compared to younger children, they would perceive more favourably an inter-ventionist mother whom Appel characterized as 'strict' and would prefer her to a mother who is permissive.

In Appel's study, middle-class children were asked to evaluate a highly permissive mother in terms of a 'good–not good' dichotomy. This mother was depicted in stories such as one in which a child is allowed to play with a friend's toy when the friend wants it back. Consistent with Appel's prediction, the majority (78.3 per cent) of 5- and 6-year-olds evaluated the mother positively as opposed to only a small minority (18.6 per cent) of 8–10-year-olds.

In support of Appel, Weisz (1980) asked older children to write essays for Mother's Day as a means of eliciting criteria for positive evaluation of mothers. The responses were categorized across a number of dimensions, one of which was 'promoting control'. It was found that, with increasing age, the presence of parental restraint was more likely to prove praiseworthy. The results were taken to be consistent with Appel's view that, as children grow older, permissive-ness is perceived less favourably.

However, in this particular study there were definite limitations. The sample was self-selected and consisted only of those children who undertook to submit the essays to a local newspaper. A prize was given for the best entry which could quite easily have affected the way the children looked upon the whole endeavour and wrote the essays. Finally, the essays focused on only the positive aspects of the mother's personality and activities.

Another study used a sample of second and fifth-graders and examined children's attitudes to both mother and father (Skeen and Gelfand 1981). Shortly before Mother's Day and Father's Day, the children were instructed to write essays on 'Why my mother is the greatest' and 'Why my father is the greatest' respectively. Again, the essays only dealt with praise of parents and were to be read by teachers and many of the parents themselves which could have had just as marked an effect as if it were a competition. As in the Appel and Weisz studies, older children made more favourable references to their parent's restrictiveness than did younger ones.

These studies are influenced by Piagetian theory. Baldwin's work provides an alternative approach which relegates egocentric responses to the realm of the non-spontaneous rather than as indicative of the child's behaviour in everyday situations. By this account (Siegal 1982, p. 70), young children have at least a tacit knowledge of others' viewpoints. Though such knowledge may not be expressed verbally in certain experimental situations, children can play and communicate effectively. In the process of parental identification and their desire to be like persons who are perceived as significant, children develop a 'consciousness of cognitions', a self-awareness of what they have in common with others. Their striving to become adult is often practised through interaction and imitation in the peer group. In this context, they may come to develop a sense of behavioural control and a rule-guided concern for others.

If children have a knowledge of others' viewpoints, they should prefer an interventionist mother. Research in naturalistic situations does indicate that intervention is often the preference of even very young children. For example, an intensive study by Bretherton and Beeghly (1982) used 30 middle-class mothers and their 28-month-old children as subjects. The mothers were asked to report on their children's utterances which referred to internal states. Contrary to any strong emphasis on egocentrism in children, a distinction between self and other was evident in their language. Words concerning moral judgement and obligation (such as, 'bad, naughty, have to, can') were applied to others before applied to the self. The results were seen as consistent with Baldwin's (1896) contention that children interpret the behaviour of others by analogy to themselves, and practise through imitation. Furthermore, a casual observation of 1- and 2-year-olds suggests that they can signal for maternal intervention when distressed by an older sibling. Thus a re-examination of the evidence taken as support for the position that young children prefer a permissive mother is needed to adjudicate the issue.

The Appel study is a good point to start. There is a possibility that the results can be attributed to a response bias artifact: that is, a tendency to describe the actions of mothers in general as 'good'. The subjects were simply asked to evaluated a permissive mother as 'good' or 'not good'. As no direct comparison was made between a permissive mother and a strict one, the children may have chosen the permissive mother as 'good' not out of egocentrism, but out of a preference for positive over negative terminology (Boucher and

Osgood 1969). We are led then to a series of studies dealing with children's perceptions of childrearing techniques.

Intervention or permissiveness?

In the first of a series of three studies designed to replicate the results of the Appel study (Siegal and Rablin 1982), the procedure was identical except that children were asked to evaluate an interventionist instead of a permissive mother. Since the outcome of this initial study might also be attributed to a response bias toward labelling an interventionist mother as 'good', a second follow-up study provided a direct comparison between interventionist and permissive mothers.

The children in both studies were aged from 4 to $5\frac{1}{2}$ years. The mean age in the first 5 years; in the second, 4 years 11 months. The children attended two preschool centres. In the first study, there were 11 girls and 9 boys; in the second, 11 of each.

The children were presented with five stories in a random order. Two of these were adapted from the examples originally provided by Appel (that is, refusing to give a toy back and throwing sand at other children). The other three involved knocking down blocks, hurting a puppy, and being rude to a grandmother. For each story in the first study, the mother told the child to stop his or her misbehaviour. The subjects were asked to judge whether that mother was 'good' or 'not good'.

The procedure of the second study was similar except that each story was accompanied by two drawings presented in a random order: one depicting the interventionist mother who told the child to stop misbehaving, and the other depicting the permissive mother who allowed the misbehaviour to continue. The children were asked to indicate which mother they preferred.

In every situation in both studies and in sharp contrast to Appel's findings, a clear majority of the children preferred the interventionist mother to the permissive one. The percentages ranged from 68 to 90. Binomial tests indicated that, apart from the children's responses in study 2 of the story about knocking down blocks, all were above chance level ($ps < 0.05$).

The two studies suggest that the Appel results may be attributable either to a response bias or perhaps to error variance. The third study was an attempt to replicate these results by testing a different group of children. Specifically, it was a test of the generality of these findings in an older age-group and across social-class membership.

A secondary purpose was to examine children's orientations toward those whose misbehaviour is allowed by mothers.

Two age-groups of 48 children participated in study 3. The younger group ranged from 4 years 10 months to 6 years 3 months (mean = 5 years 4 months), and the older group from 7 years 10 months to 8 years 11 months (mean = 8 years 5 months). Half the children in each group were from upper-middle class families with fathers engaged in managerial or professional occupations. The other half were from working-class families.

The five situations and pairs of drawings were the same as those in study 2. As before, the children were asked whether they preferred the permissive or the interventionist mother. The child in the story was the same sex as the subject.

Two additional questions were asked in order to ascertain whether or not the child regarded intervention as an arbitrary act having no more consequence than non-intervention. The subjects were told, 'One child stops because his mother told him to. The other child doesn't stop and his mother didn't ask him to stop.' They were then asked, 'Is one child naughtier than the other or are they both the same?' This question was followed by a third to determine whether the subjects' judgements on the five situations could be regarded as moral ones, in the sense that they were generalizable across varying patterns of mother–child relationships: 'Suppose mothers didn't mind if children (would not give other children's toys back, etc.). Would it be right or wrong to do it then?' As in the original Appel (1977) study, justifications were sought to supplement the subjects' choices.

The vast majority of children consistently indicated a preference for the interventionist mother. Out of the 96 children, 68 chose the interventionist mother on all five situations, and 19 on four out of the five. Only four children chose this mother on three situations, four on two, and one child on one situation. With regard to the consequences of non-intervention, 82 out of the 96 children on all five situations claimed that the child who continued the behaviour was naughtier. Similarly, 82 out of 96 claimed that it would be wrong to so behave if mothers did not mind.

Almost all children regardless of age, sex, or social class consistently responded that, even if mothers in general did not mind, it would be wrong to behave in the same way as the children depicted in the five situations. Their transgressions were construed as moral ones which are intrinsically wrong rather than ones defined as wrong through particular social conventions. Virtually all of the justifications for (a) preferring the interventionist mother, (b) choosing the child who continued to behave as naughtier, and (c) responding that in the absence of sanctions such behaviour would be wrong either focused on the consequences of these actions for others or the importance of children's self-adherence to rules.

The form of preferred intervention

If children at an early age advocate intervention to stop misbehaviour what kind of intervention is preferred?

One of the most frequently used classifications of childrearing methods has been that described by Hoffman (1970). He sees socialization behaviour as falling into three types: power-assertion, love-withdrawal, and induction.

Power-assertive techniques consist of physical punishment or force, deprivation of material objects, or any other technique that includes displays of the superior physical power of the parent in maintaining control over the child. The main rationale for using this form of discipline is that the child will be too scared of pain or physical deprivation to repeat this misdeed.

Love-withdrawal does not involve physical discipline but uses the child's fear in the same fashion. It involves expressing one's disapproval of the child in non-physical, emotional ways. For example, the child may be ignored by the parent or told that he or she is not loved anymore. Demonstrations of love-withdrawal are designed to make the child afraid of losing parental love and nurturance. This technique is far less concrete and definite in quality than power-assertion and can be confusing for a young child who does not realize that the parent is usually withdrawing his love only temporarily. In psychoanalytical terms, this form of discipline engenders high guilt feelings and insecurities, and encourages the development of an advanced superego.

The third type of parental discipline, induction, uses explanations to demonstrate to children why they have misbehaved and the effect that their behaviour has on others in order to convince children to change in future. Discipline is not designed to punish the child emotionally or physically, but is directed towards the child's cognitive abilities to see the need for acting in accordance with the parent's wishes. Identification with the mother, as shown on the Hoffman (1971) index, has been found to be significantly related to her use of induction (Hoffman and Saltzstein 1967).

A subsequent study (Siegal and Cowen 1984) was designed to

examine the conditions under which children with increasing age advocate elements of power-assertion (in this case, physical punishment), withdrawal of love, and induction in maternal childrearing techniques. One purpose was to examine whether children's evaluations are determined more by the behaviour of the mother in particular situations than by a consistent orientation toward childrearing on the part of the child. The children may be enamoured of a mother who is flexible and varies her reactions to misbehaviour. Alternatively, they may have a global, undifferentiated outlook and view, for example, induction or affect-laden reasoning as appropriate regardless of the situation. As there is a lack of evidence which bears on this issue, no predictions were made as to the comparative strengths of situations, mothers, and subjects as determinants of evaluations.

Another purpose was to examine the nature of children's disciplinary preferences. Several studies are pertinent here. According to Piaget (1977*b*), younger children believe that transgressors receive harsh punishments in order to feel the weight of adult authority. Older children are more likely to maintain that the punishment should fit the crime and to understand the meaning of induction (Mancuso and Allen 1976). Moreover, children with increasing age are more likely to respond to other-oriented appeals to obey (LaVoie 1974). On this basis, it was expected that younger children should approve of physical reprimands while older children would be more likely to approve of induction. Even so, as shown by the Siegal and Rablin studies, children regardless of age should generally prefer some form of intervetion to permissiveness.

A further aim was to compare ratings of different techniques. Guided by the research on authoritative parenting (Baumrind 1973), it has been suggested that the most effective parent who has obedient children employs induction backed up by the occasional use of power assertion (Henry 1980; Zahn-Waxler, Radke-Yarrow, and King 1979). Since obedience should be mediated by positive evaluations of mothers' discipline techniques, it was anticipated that power-assertion would be mildly approved as compared to induction which would receive stronger approval.

Five age groups of children participated in the study, each consisting of ten boys and ten girls. The youngest group attended preschool and ranged from 4 years 10 months to 6 years 2 months (mean = 5 years 9 months). The other groups attended grades 3, 6, 9, and 12. Their age ranges (with means shown in parentheses) were 8 years 2 months to 9 years 8 months (8 years 9 months), 10 years 8 months to 12 years 3 months (11 years 9 months), 13 years

8 months to 15 years 6 months (14 years 7 months), and 16 years
9 months to 18 years 8 months (17 years 8 months).

The children were given five common situations in which a
4–5-year-old was described as having committed a transgression.
These were patterned after the five categories used by Grusec and
Kuczynski (1980, p. 3):

(a) Simple disobedience: A child refuses a mother's request to
     clean up a bedroom.
(b) Disobedience causing physical harm to others: a child is
     punched by another and the child's ice-cream is taken away.
(c) Disobedience causing physical harm to the self: after being told
     by the mother not to touch a stove, the child touches it anyway
     and is burnt.
(d) Disobedience causing psychological harm to others: a child
     laughs at another child who falls from crutches.
(e) Disobedience causing harm to physical objects: a child knows
     that it is wrong to skip in the lounge but does so anyway and
     breaks a lamp.

After each story, four possible disciplinary reactions on the part of
the mother were listed. The children were asked to rate the mother's
behaviour on a five-point rating scale ranging from 'very good' to
'very bad'. The types of disciplinary reactions were patterned after
Hoffman's classification): (1) the mother slapped her child for misbehaving (physical punishment); (2) the mother would not talk to
the child for the rest of the day (withdrawal of love); (3) the mother
explained the consequences of the child's actions, pointing out the
effects on the child and others (induction); and (4) the mother did
not intervene, believing that the child would learn to behave independently (permissiveness).

The situations and techniques were presented to all the subjects in
a random order. The preschoolers were seen individually by a
female experimenter and told that they would hear some stories
about four different children and their mothers. All four would be
doing the same thing. But each mother would do different things to
get her child to stop. They were then shown five faces which represented a rating scale from very wrong (big scowl), wrong (frown),
half right–half wrong (neutral expression), right (smile), and very
right (big grin). The subjects were read each story and then presented with the actions of the four mothers illustrated by a series of
line drawings. They were told to say how right each of the mothers
was to do what she did by pointing at one of the faces.

The same procedure was followed for half the third-graders. The other half received the situations and techniques in a questionnaire format in which they were instructed to circle their responses on a 0–4 scale. There were no significant differences between responses in the two modes and all subjects in grades 6, 9, and 12 were given the items on a questionnaire format.

There were 20 items in total, producing evaluations of four mothers over five situations. For example, on the broken lamp situation, the subjects were to evaluate a mother who explained that the lamp was needed to use in the room and that she was upset at its breakage and the trouble it would take to get it fixed (induction). The other three mothers were described as hitting the child (physical punishment), refusing to talk to the child (love-withdrawal), and deciding not to do anything with the belief that the child would learn independently (permissiveness).

The results (Table 4.1) clearly indicated that children's responses were influenced by the range of situations. With increasing age, all childrearing techniques were evaluated generally less favourably, but children of all ages and on all five situations preferred induction. Physical punishment was next popular but grew increasingly out of favour by grade 12. Permissiveness was generally rated unfavourably except in the stove incident involving physical harm to oneself, for which it was at times claimed that a child who was stupid enough to do it once would learn by his or her mistake. For preschoolers and third-graders, withdrawal of love was seen to be intermediary in effectiveness between power assertion and permissiveness whereas older children generally did not distinguish love-withdrawal from permissiveness. Thus a major concern which appears to be uppermost in children's evaluations of maternal socialization behaviour appears to be the degree and form of control.

Reciprocal influence and the meaning of control

Even young children appear to advocate intervention over permissiveness. The form of preferred intervention is dominated by induction and backed up by power assertion in the form of physical punishment. Permissiveness and withdrawal of love, which may be construed by children as a type of permissiveness, are far behind. As in other attempts to elicit children's reports of parental behaviour (Armentrout and Burger 1972; Burger and Armentrout 1971; Schaefer 1965a and b), the key issue which emerges is whether

Table 4.1 Ratings of techniques and situations: means and standard deviations (from Siegal and Cowen 1984)

| | | Techniques | | | | | | | | | | | | | | | | | | | |
| | | Induction | | | | | Physical punishment | | | | | Love withdrawal | | | | | Permissiveness | | | | |
Situation:		SID	PHO	PHS	PSHO	DCHP	SID	PHO	PHS	PSHO	DCHP	SID	PHO	PHS	PSHO	DCHP	SID	PHO	PHS	PSHO	DCHP
Group preschool	M	3.70	3.95	3.80	3.55	3.70	3.35	3.55	3.05	3.20	3.60	1.75	1.90	1.95	2.20	2.05	0.95	0.45	0.35	0.25	1.05
(M age = 5 years 9 months)	SD	0.71	0.21	0.68	0.92	0.71	1.19	0.92	1.36	1.29	0.92	1.81	1.67	1.80	1.66	1.83	1.36	0.74	0.73	0.43	1.53
Grade 3	M	3.80	3.65	3.70	3.70	3.10	3.25	3.30	2.35	3.45	3.15	2.40	1.90	1.80	1.45	1.95	0.90	0.40	0.40	0.40	0.75
(M age = 8 years 9 months)	SD	0.40	0.65	0.64	0.46	0.77	0.99	0.90	1.53	0.92	1.11	1.39	1.34	1.33	1.40	1.47	1.09	0.92	0.66	0.66	0.94
Grade 6	M	3.30	3.45	3.45	3.55	2.80	2.45	2.65	1.90	3.15	2.65	0.95	0.95	0.95	0.90	1.10	1.30	0.50	1.45	0.75	1.50
(M age = 11 years 9 months)	SD	0.64	0.59	0.50	0.92	0.93	0.92	0.91	1.37	0.85	0.85	0.97	1.07	0.86	1.14	1.14	1.38	0.81	0.97	0.94	0.92
Grade 9	M	2.60	3.05	3.15	3.50	2.70	2.85	2.55	1.50	2.60	2.70	0.65	0.50	0.90	0.80	0.80	1.00	0.45	1.70	0.35	0.65
(M age = 14 years 7 months)	SD	0.80	0.80	0.57	0.50	0.95	0.96	0.97	0.87	0.92	0.90	0.65	0.67	1.09	0.98	0.87	1.00	0.59	1.19	0.48	0.73
Grade 12	M	2.60	3.30	2.85	3.55	2.80	2.15	1.95	1.50	1.70	1.95	0.40	0.55	0.50	0.40	0.70	0.80	0.30	1.40	0.30	0.70
(M age = 17 years 8 months)	SD	1.02	0.84	1.06	0.74	1.03	1.28	1.28	1.25	1.27	1.16	0.49	0.74	0.59	0.73	1.01	1.08	0.56	1.07	0.71	0.71

The situations were: SID—simple disobedience, PHO—disobedience causing physical harm to others, PHS—disobedience causing physical harm to self, PHSO—disobedience causing psychological harm to others, and DCHP—disobedience causing harm to physical objects. Responses are distributed on a five-point scale: 0 = very wrong, 1 = wrong, 2 = half-right, half-wrong, 3 = right, 4 = very right.

parental socialization behaviour implies acceptance or rejection of the child.

Advocacy of both power assertion and induction parallels some important work on the effectiveness of various childrearing techniques. For example, in one study (Zahn-Waxler, Radke-Yarrow, and King 1979), the mothers of children aged $1\frac{1}{2}$–$2\frac{1}{2}$ years were trained in observation techniques. They were asked to record their own reactions to their child's misbehaviour (such as hitting innocent playmates) and his or her subsequent reparations. The mothers' use of inductive statements delivered clearly and often with 'emotional investment' were most predictive of reparation on the part of the children. Moreover, such 'moralizing' correlated with the use of physical punishment, indicating that reasoning and power are useful childrearing methods for young children.

The nature of evaluations, as situationally determined, may therefore be seen as manifestations of an implicit theory of childrearing which is evident early in social development. Authoritative parenting demands both firmness and flexibility to deal with the situation at hand. Effective socialization may be promoted by the degree to which children perceive a high degree of legitimized control underlying their parents' interventions. Sensitivity to the demands of the situation may convey to children a sense of parents' concern for their welfare. A dual process of effective control may consist of salient techniques employed together with subtlety in the form of flexibility. Salience may produce external attributions and flexibility internal ones, and a balance between the two may relate to both maternal identification and behavioural development.

As in previous studies, young children were not afraid of evaluating adults negatively. However, with increasing age, positive evaluations of the actions of all mothers declined in general. This finding is compatible with Piaget's contention (1977*b*) that a unilateral respect for adults gives way as children grow older. Even so, in relative terms of adulation, the authoritative parent remains superior to the one who uses love-withdrawal or permissiveness.

Plainly, there are many variants of induction (Hoffman 1970, p. 286). More subtle inductive techniques, not presented to children here, may be evaluated no less or even more favourably with age. Indeed, the situations and techniques presented to the children in this study were not so comprehensive as to include the different shades of misbehaviour and childrearing methods which occur in everyday life. Power assertion, for example, can involve physical isolation and threats as well as physical punishment. One avenue for future research is to examine evaluations of situations as handled by the many techniques often subsumed under broader classifications.

The method of having children evaluate, rather than enumerate, a range of childrearing strategies permits a comparison of pre-schoolers' responses with those of older children. Nevertheless, there are several other limitations to this study. The children were asked to evaluate only mothers' behaviour and not fathers', and evaluations of fathers may differ considerably (see, for example, Kagan and Lemkin 1960). The situations were restricted to young culprits only. Evaluations of how older children might be handled may have differed, and may as well be influenced by the gender of the culprit.

Bearing such limitations in mind, the results are in keeping with recent critiques of Piaget's notion of egocentrism. But even if the child can in some sense be termed egocentric, these studies are not necessarily germane to egocentrism as defined by Piaget. While Piaget maintained that young children cannot take the role of the other, he also claimed that they judge acts out of a rigid, unilateral respect for adult rules. Young children are said to advocate that transgressors who violate rules should feel the full weight of adult authority: 'The fairest punishment will be the most severe' (Piaget 1977*b*, p. 205). A preference for an interventionist mother over a permissive one might in fact be more consistent with Piaget's position.

Indirectly, these studies also underscore the importance of exploring reciprocal influences in socialization (Bell 1968; Bell and Harper 1977). As Bandura (1978, 1983) points out, parent–child relations can be viewed in a context of reciprocal determinism. Neither the behaviour of child culprits nor the socialization be-haviours of mothers can be regarded as dependent variables but as interlocking determinant of each other. Mothers' childrearing prac-tices alter children's behaviour, and children's behaviour alters mothers' childrearing practices. To view parent–child relations as reciprocally influenced entails that attention be focused not only on the mother's reactions to children's misbehaviour but on children's evaluations of the mother which, especially in the case of girls, may guide their subsequent behaviour.

To address the issue of whether the individuality of the child, the type of technique used by the mother, or the nature of the situation in which the culprit has misbehaved determines evaluations of disci-pline techniques, the data in the Siegal and Cowen (1984) study were reanalysed in components analyses of variance (Endler 1966;

Endler and Hunt 1968) performed separately for each of the five age groups with children (subjects), techniques, and situations as factors. For each analysis, the misbehaviours × techniques interaction was found to account for 18–20 per cent of the variance in evaluations as compared to the children × techniques interaction which accounted for 12–14 per cent. The technique used by the mother determine evaluations somewhat more than the nature of the children themselves. Yet the effects can be viewed as bidirectional since evaluations were determined by the technique employed by the mother in interaction first, with the type of situation and, second, with the nature of the child making the evaluation. Thus evaluations can be characterized in terms of a transactional process to which the culprit's misbehaviour, the mother's discipline technique and the nature of the child making the evaluation all contribute. Over 30 per cent of the variance in evaluations came from the two simple first-order interactions, influences which will be explored further in Chapter 8 of this volume. Caution, however, is warranted in interpreting these results. The more divergent the situations, the more responses may be attributed to situational effects rather than to consistent response modes on the part of subjects (Mischel 1968).

Intervention in the enforcement of moral rules and social conventions

That the form of preferred intervention varies with the situation leads to a consideration of how the message transmitted by parents in practised in social interaction. Turiel's (1978, 1983a and b) distinction between moral rules and social conventions is relevant here, for peers and adults respond to, and conceive of, moral rules and social conventions in different ways. The latter are arbitrary and defined with reference to a particular social setting. Rule transgressions are evaluated as wrong depending upon whether they occur in this setting. Outside the relevant context, such acts are no longer evaluated as naughty. Children may claim that standing during snack time is naughty in a school where this is against the rules, but not naughty in a school which has no such rule.

Moral rules are not arbitrary and are not tied to social contexts. Moral rule transgressions are intrinsically wrong regardless of whether a social rule exists. Children may claim that fighting is naughty even in a place which has no rule against fighting, and that authorities should prevent such incidents despite the non-existence of a rule in a particular context (Weston and Turiel 1980).

The ability of children aged 5 years and under to distinguish between the two rule domains has been shown in behavioural observations and in studies of children's conceptual understanding. An initial behavioural study (Nucci and Turiel 1978) consisted of observations of children in ten preschools in the Santa Cruz, California, area. Events in the preschool were classified as social conventional transgressions (such as engaging in work or play activities in other than designated areas or time periods) or moral transgressions involving the welfare of others (such as intentionally hitting others, taking what belongs to another, and failing to share with others).

Both the children's and teachers' responses to social and moral transgressions were scored according to the criteria shown in Table 4.2. Children and adults responded with equal frequency to moral

Table 4.2   Definitions of response categories
(from Nucci and Turiel 1978, p. 403)

Injury or loss statement	Statements indicating pain or injury to self or personal loss (loss of property, personal space, etc.).
Emotional exclamation of response	Statement expressing emotional state or exclamation of effect.
Providing rationale	Reason(s) given for a rule or behaviour.
Feelings of others	Statements by others pointing to the feelings of the victim; telling victim of transgression to express feelings to transgressor or telling transgressor how it feels to be the victim of the act.
Physical response	Any physical act taken toward the transgressor.
Involve adult	Request for adult intervention, or statement by a child to an adult describing the misbehaviour of another, or threat to tell adult of another's misbehaviour.
Disorder statement	Indication that behaviour is creating a mess, disorder, or chaos.
Rule statement	Statements specifying a rule governing the action.
Sanction statement	Statement indicating that a sanction will be the response to the behaviour.
Command	To do or cease from doing an act, without a statement of rule.

transgressions. Adults provided a rationale, and pointed out the feelings of a victim; children responded with a loss or injury statement, an emotional reaction, a physical response, a command, or a request for adult intervention. By contrast, only adults responded to social conventional transgressions with commands, disorder, rule, or sanction statements. Similar findings have come from other studies (Nucci and Nucci 1982; Smetana 1983).

Children's inattention to social conventional transgressions may be due to their perception of such transgressions as less serious and deserving of less punishment than moral rule transgressions. Smetana (1981) presented preschoolers with two groups of items: moral (one child hitting another, a child not sharing a toy, a child shoving another, a child throwing water at another, and a child taking another's apple) and social-conventional (a child not participating in show and tell; a child not sitting in the designated place on a rug during story time, a child not saying grace before a snack, a child putting a toy away in the incorrect place, and a child not placing belongings in the designated place). The preschoolers responded that, compared to the moral rule transgressions, social-conventional transgressions are less serious, merit less punishment, and would even be all right if there were no rule or in a different context altogether.

These results have been interpreted to place in doubt aspects of traditional cognitive-developmental approaches to socialization. For Piaget (1977*b*), the heteronomous morality of the young child precludes a distinction between social and moral rules; from the child's unilateral respect perspective, rule transgressions in either domain are regarded as naughty for they are contrary to adult authority.

While Piaget contended that mature conceptions of rules are constructed from peer-oriented social interactions, Turiel (1978, 1983*a* and *b*) has proposed that this distinction arises from qualitatively different aspects of the individual's social interactions as adults have been shown to respond differently to social conventional and moral transgressions. Moreover, adults, rather than peers, initiate responses to transgressions against social rules (Nucci and Nucci 1982; Nucci and Turiel 1978).

However, as Shweder (1982) comments, the source of children's understanding remains unclear. In this regard, the data which Piaget used to support his claim came from children living in the poorer parts of Swiss cities who were unlikely to have been exposed to intensive peer-group influence at the age of 5 years and under. Such exposure, for example, is given to children who attend daycare centres on a full-time basis. That these children distinguish between social and moral rules can be interpreted as consistent with Piaget's theory.

Though Smetana (1981) found that preschool children aged $2\frac{1}{2}$–$4\frac{1}{2}$ years discriminate between rules in the two domains, the degree to which the children were previously exposed to social inter- action was not examined. Though 'exceedingly little' is known about the effects of daycare (Belsky and Steinberg 1978; Belsky, Steinberg, and Walker 1982), there is evidence, albeit equivocal, which sug- gests that daycare children are more peer-oriented than children who do not attend daycare (Moore, 1975; Schwarz, Krolick, and Strickland 1973) and that daycare children are more non-compliant with adult directives (Rubenstein, Howes, and Boyle 1981).

Should daycare children differ from others in judging social rule violations less severely and in distinguishing between social and moral transgressions, it may be because they are exposed to permis- sive adult caretakers who practise less authoritative childcare prac- tices than do parents at home. However, such an interpretation would appear somewhat unlikely. Despite wide variations in child- rearing methods, there are few differences in judgements of trans- gressions among abused, neglected, and non-maltreated children (Smetana, Kelly, and Twentyman 1984). Moreover, as already noted, whether or not caregiving is firm and authoritative, the child's understanding of rules may reflect perceptions of control and a willingness to obey. Adults' verbal reactions to preschoolers' social and moral transgressions may differ (Nucci and Turiel 1978) but they are interventions all the same. These may set the stage for dif- ferences in the quality of social interaction which are imperceptible when compared to the behaviour of peers who rarely respond to social transgressions at all and may in fact condone such actions.

The effects of daycare were explored in two recent studies (Siegal and Storey in press). Both were guided by a social-cognitive hypo- thesis. Though Piaget posited that preschool-aged children do not have the cognitive skills to be influenced by social interaction, it was expected that daycare veterans will be more likely than their newly enrolled counterparts to identify social rule transgressions as viola- tions against conventions in contrast to the intrinsic wrongness of transgressions against moral rules.

Daycare and children's social knowledge

Subjects in the first study consisted of two groups of ten boys and ten girls each. One group had attended the same childcare centre for 18 months or more from 9 a.m. to 5 p.m. at least 3 full days a week. Their mean age was 4 years 4 months (range = 3 years 8 months to 5 years 1 month). They had been in care for a mean of 2 years 6 months (range = 1 year 6 months to 3 years 6 months). The second group had been newly enrolled for the past 3 months in the same centres attended by the daycare veterans. Their mean age was 4 years 3 months (range = 3 years 7 months to 5 years 2 months). No child in the group had had previous daycare or preschool experience.

At the time of testing, both groups attended preschool programmes. These were continuations of daycare programmes for 2 and 3-year-olds and were held within the same buildings. Both programmes were government subsidized. In daycare, the children participated in groups of six to ten peers of a similar age supervised by two adults; in preschool, the group size was the same and supervision was carried out by only one adult.

The parents of all the children were engaged in professional occupations mainly as physicians, lawyers, computer scientists, and university lecturers. Both mothers and fathers had a post-secondary education. It can be assumed that the two groups of children did not have parents who differed in their attitudes toward daycare. Parents of newly enrolled children previously had had their children on a waiting list for daycare for between 10 and 24 months. They were unable earlier to meet the enrolment quotas imposed by the centres because the family had recently moved into the area and/or did not have access to information about the demand for daycare services.

The children were given the moral and social rule items used by Smetana (1981) closely following the same procedure. Some terms were changed to conform with Australian usage (for example, 'kindy' for 'kindergarten'), and one social conventional item, 'a child not saying grace before meals' was changed to 'a child eating ice-cream with a fork' to ensure familiarity. Other social stimuli involved incidents such as a child not putting a toy away in the correct spot; the moral stimuli involved incidents such as a child hitting another child. For each stimulus item, the subjects were asked to point to a scale of four faces in order to indicate the naughtiness of the transgression. As in the Smetana study, a series of four faces were depicted with progressively larger and more exaggerated frowns and verbally labelled to indicate that the transgressor was 'OK' (happy face), 'a little bit bad', 'very bad', or 'very, very bad' (big scowl). Before using the scale, all the subjects demonstrated that they could correctly identify each scale point by pointing to the appropriate face. Responses were recorded on a four-point scale from (1) OK to (4) very, very bad. Subjects were then asked, 'Do you think the child should get into trouble?' and if so, 'A little or a lot?' Responses were coded on a three-point scale which ranged from (0) 'no' to (2) 'a lot'.

The results supported the social-cognitive hypothesis. Compared to children who had newly been enrolled, daycare veterans differentiated more between moral and social rules. On basically the same set of items in the Smetana study, they judged social rule transgressions as less naughty and as less worthy of punishment than did the newly enrolled children who in turn did not discriminate between the amount of punishment due to transgressions against moral and social rules.

The initial study was restricted to comparisons of the perceived naughtiness and punishment due to moral and social transgressions. A second study was undertaken in an attempt to replicate partially the initial findings. As well, the study aimed to examine the effects of daycare on children's conceptions of moral and social rules as contingent upon a particular setting. It was predicted that daycare veterans would be more likely than their newly enrolled counterparts to distinguish the arbitrary nature of social rules as opposed to prescriptive nature of moral rules. Also, they would be more likely to prefer teacher intervention in moral transgressions rather than social ones, and to indicate that moral rather than social transgressions would still be wrong regardless of whether teachers minded or not.

There was a further aim underlying the second study. According to Piaget, the heteronomous morality of the young child is characterized by a unilateral respect orientation. The criterion by which actions are judged as wrong is that adult authority is violated. There is an inability to take the role of the disadvantaged other who accidentally may violate adult rules. Through increased social interaction, children become less egocentric and a concern with others' welfare supplants adult authority as a criterion for judging actions. Thus, the newly enrolled, who are less advanced in their conceptions of moral and social rules, should be more egocentric in their judgements of rule transgressions.

Another possibility is that the daycare child is simply more familiar with social transgressions. According to Davidson, Turiel, and Black (1983), children's conceptions of rules are constructed from prior experiences. It would follow that veterans' responses should differ from the newly enrolled on this dimension as well, providing a basis for explaining differences between the groups in rule conceptions. Alternatively, the groups may be equally familiar with rules since both have attended daycare for 3 months. But the veterans' extended exposure to peers and daycare workers provides a source for 'socially constructed knowledge', defined by Shweder (1982, p. 55) as 'knowledge that one acquires with the assistance of previously organized, preregulated, prepackaged "collective representations"'. Without stimulating a cooperative coordination of others' perspectives or increasing children's familiarity with rules, a knowledge of the moral and social rule domains may be transmitted to the child within the daycare setting. Newly enrolled children may not yet have acquired a prepackaged representation of rules.

To explore these possibilities, subjects in the second study were given an additional set of questions which pertained to familiarity and egocentrism in children's conceptions of rule transgressions.

The social experience of daycare as a force underlying adult–child relations: a social-cognitive analysis

The criteria for selecting the subjects were identical to those used for the first study. Again two groups of ten boys and ten girls each were tested. The mean age of the veterans was 4 years 1 month (range = 2 years 11 months to 5 years 3 months) and that of the newly enrolled was 4 years 2 months (3 years 1 month to 5 years 5 months).

The subjects were presented with three moral and three social rule transgressions. The three moral transgressions consisted of (1) a child hitting another child, (2) a child not sharing a toy, and (3) a child not helping another child who trips in the playground, an item which was not included in the first study.

Following the distinction made by Tisak and Ford (1983), the first involves an intentionally produced negative consequence (active morality), the second involves a non-equitable distribution of resources, and the third involves a negative reaction to a mishap. These categories encompass events which have unique elements with regard to initiating, refraining from or responding to a victimizing act. Thus this study sought to broaden examination of children's conceptions of moral rules beyond active morality and distribution of resources to include responses to mishaps.

The three social transgressions consisted of (4) a child not putting a toy away in the correct spot, (5) a child not sitting at story time, and (6) a child eating ice-cream with a fork instead of a spoon. These transgressions were chosen as the ones of most interest to the subjects in the first study.

The children were asked twelve questions for each transgression. Questions 1 and 2 on perceived naughtiness and punishment due were the same as in the first study and were scored in the same way. Questions 3 and 4 concerned rule contingency and relatively. Using the hitting situation to illustrate, subjects were asked: '(3) Would hitting be OK if the child wouldn't get into trouble for hitting? (4) Would it be OK to hit other children at home or in another kindy?'

The next two questions concerned conceptions of rules in relation to adult authority. In order to facilitate attention, the subjects were shown Lego figures representing two teachers and two children. In the hitting example they were told 'Look at these two children. Both were hitting. This child was told to stop by that teacher. That child was also hitting and was not told to stop by the teacher.' The subjects were then asked: '(5) Which teacher do you like better? The one who asked the child to stop or the teacher who didn't ask the child to stop? (6) Suppose teachers didn't mind if children hit other children. Would hitting be right or wrong then?'

Questions 7, 8, and 9 concerned the familiarity of the situation. These were taken from the study of Davidson, Turiel, and Black (1983): '(7) Do you know anyone who got into trouble for hitting? (8) Have you ever heard of it happening? (9) Have you ever got into trouble for hitting?'

The last three questions on egocentrism were adapted from a study by Smetana, Kelly, and Twentyman (1984). Half the subjects in each group (five boys and five girls) were asked these questions as if they applied to themselves. The other half were given the questions as if they applied to someone else. As earlier, the subjects were presented with the row of four faces and asked: '(10) Point to the face which tells how bad it is for you/someone else to hit. (11) Should the teacher be cross with you/them? A little or a lot? (12) Would it be all right for you/anyone else to hit if the teacher didn't get cross?' The term 'cross' was particularly familiar to the children, and one which did not necessarily connote punishment. It was used instead of 'get in trouble' to compare answers to questions 11 and 12 with those given to questions 2 and 3. Mean scores are shown in Table 4.3.

On questions 1, 3, 4, 5, 6, 10, 11, and 12 the veterans more sharply differentiated between moral and social rules than did the newly enrolled. Compared to the newly enrolled, the veterans differentiated moral from social transgressions as naughtier and worse,

Table 4.3 Mean scores on the six items used in the second daycare study (Siegal and Storey in press)

	Item						Questions						
		1	2	3	4	5	6	7	8	9	10	11	12
Veterans													
Moral	1	3.65	1.90	0.80	1.00	0.85	0.90	0.80	0.85	0.30	3.30	0.85	0.80
	2	3.20	1.90	0.65	0.70	0.70	0.85	0.65	0.70	0.30	3.25	1.00	0.65
	3	3.45	1.45	0.60	0.80	0.85	0.80	0.60	0.70	0.30	3.40	0.95	0.65
Social	4	2.10	0.95	0.20*	0.65	0.55	0.25*	0.60	0.55	0.25*	2.35	0.50*	0.15*
	5	2.45	1.10	0.25*	0.30*	0.70	0.45	0.50	0.65	0.10*	2.35	0.45*	0.30*
	6	1.50*	0.90	0.45	0.60	0.40	0.20*	0.45	0.35	0.05*	2.00	0.55*	0.15*
Newly enrolled													
Moral	1	3.25	1.60	0.70	0.80	0.55	0.70	0.70	0.55	0.35	3.55	1.20	0.50
	2	3.25	1.55	0.45	0.75	0.55	0.80	0.75	0.75	0.30	3.75	1.05	0.70
	3	3.20	1.10	0.60	0.75	0.75	0.55	0.60	0.60	0.25*	3.00	0.75	0.65
Social	4	3.00	0.80	0.60	0.85	0.65	0.70	0.60	0.70	0.35	2.85	0.80	0.65
	5	3.40	0.95	0.65	0.55	0.70	0.80	0.55	0.50	0.20*	3.15	0.80	0.55
	6	3.50	1.20	0.60	0.55	0.70	0.70	0.40	0.35	0.20*	3.30	1.10	0.50

Items 1, 2, and 3 refer to hitting, not sharing, and not helping. Items 4, 5, and 6 refer to not putting a toy away, not sitting, and eating ice-cream with a fork. Scores above chance ($p < 0.05$ by one-tailed binomial tests) are underlined; below-chance scores are marked by asterisks. Answers to questions 1 and 10 were scored on a 1–4 scale, answers to 2 and 11 were scored on a 0–2 scale, and all others on a 0–1 scale.

wrong even if there was no punishment, worthier of adult intervention and anger, and wrong even if teachers did not or would not get
cross.

Unlike in the first study, there were no differences in the groups'
conceptions of rule violations meriting punishment. Consistent with
Tisak and Ford's assertion that active morality is distinguishable
from prosocial behaviour, hitting was judged to be somewhat more
worthy of punishment than not sharing or not helping. In any event,
transgressions may be expressed in terms of an adult becoming cross
rather than a child receiving punishment, and in this case the differences between the groups were significant.

Responses on questions 7 and 8 indicated that moral transgressions were generally perceived as more familiar than the social transgressions. Only on question 11 was there evidence of egocentrism
with both veterans and the newly enrolled claiming that the teacher
should be more cross with others' transgressions than their own.

Daycare has a significant effect on children's conceptions of social
rules which is not related to egocentrism or a lack of stimulus familiarity. Across a range of situations, moral transgressions are regarded
as equally serious by veterans and newly enrolled alike while the distinction between morality and convention is unclear for the newly
enrolled.

Daycare veterans prefer adults to be discriminating in their interventions. They have more highly developed expectations of the use
of adult authority, and prefer that it be exercised in moral rather
than social situations. The finding of Rubenstein, Howes, and Boyle
(1981) that daycare children are less compliant with adult directives
can be readily interpreted in this light. Here parent–child interactions were observed in game-like situations in which the child was
asked to adhere to social conventions. If social transgressions are
regarded by veterans as relatively acceptable, conflict can ensue
which is not present in the parent–child interactions of newly
enrolled children who have had more limited social experience. In
this sense, the daycare child may exert more influence on the parent's
behaviour than does the newly enrolled.

That daycare children are exposed to more adults as well as more
peers might mean that the adults are providing veterans with experiences upon which to construct conceptions of social rules. Yet while
daycare workers may be more lenient than parents in dealing with
child misdemeanours (Hess *et al.* 1981), it must be reiterated that
they respond to both moral and social transgressions by intervention. Peers, however, ignore transgressions viewed as social in

nature. Therefore, children's knowledge of social conventions is more likely to be gained, as Piaget originally proposed, through peer-group interaction. At the least, these results serve to roll back somewhat the doubt cast on Piaget's proposition that young children without peer-group exposure have an undifferentiated, global outlook on adult rules. But according to a Piagetian interpretation, the newly enrolled should have been more egocentric than the veterans in their judgements of rule transgressions. This was not the case and, although the measures themselves may not have been sensitive enough to detect differences, the two groups responded similarly to the questions on familiarity as well.

Thus Shweder's suggestion receives support: young children may receive conceptions of social rules through social rather than self-construction processes. These may be pre-packaged entities which the child comes to embrace with increasing peer-group exposure. The relation between children's social interaction and their orientation to rules is liable to be extremely complex. It may be that unpopular or rejected children approach all rules, whether moral or social, in a negative way. Furman and Masters (1980) found that preschoolers disliked by their peers deviated more in situations where a prohibition to play with a toy was purportedly endorsed either by an adult or a peer. In a study by Coie, Dodge, and Coppetelli (1982), disliked primary school children were rated by their peers as those who both disrupt the group and get into trouble with their teachers.

Theoretical implications

In line with the original Baldwin position (1896, p. 17), children generally may learn rules from adults through active 'affective-conative strivings'. Rule-guided behaviour may be practised in the peer group where it undergoes modifications leading to a consciousness of cognitions—in this case, relations between rules and behaviours in their social contexts. Children can come to reflect on the applicability of rules to themselves and others through the social knowledge gained in peer-group interaction. They come to internalize rules for behaviour and follow these even when external surveillance is withdrawn. Familiarity alone is not enough to guarantee that children distinguish between social and moral rules. The type of social experience upon which familiarity is based must also be considered.

The parent's discipline techniques may enter into identificatory processes which make a parallel independent contribution to behaviour. As Hoffman (1970, p. 306) has conceded,

Quite apart from its psychoanalytic origins, it makes good sense logically to assume that some process such as identification operates in moral development. Why should a person criticize and blame himself for not behaving in accord with the standards of another person even in that person's absence, unless he has somehow come to adopt the latter's evaluative role and no longer views his behavior solely in terms of its relevance to impulse gratification?

In this social–cognitive analysis of identification and internalized behaviour, young children appraise parents' sensitivity to situations positively. The notion of egocentrism is not accurate. A knowledge of morality and convention is acquired through a wide range of social experience. Perceptions of the legitimacy of parental control, together with the nature of peer-group interaction, influence children's understanding of rules.

Salient firm control without flexibility may produce external attributions on the part of the child, and flexible reactions from both parents and peers may lead to internal attributions. In eliciting internalized behaviour, salient control through the reinforcements and punishments prescribed by social learning theorists may be appropriate for young children. With increasing age, subtle control based on attribution theory may be more effective. Strong support for age differences in the relationship between types of attributions and children's behaviour and understanding of parental influence techniques is still lacking (Dalenberg, Bierman, and Furman 1984; Dix and Grusec 1983; Perry and Perry 1983, p. 130; Siegal 1982, pp. 114–16). However, as will be seen, tentative evidence does exist which is contingent upon children's perceptions of parents' expectations and socialization behaviours.

The mix of control techniques may vary with the nature of the situation, the individual child, and the mother and father as immersed in a socioeconomic context. The next step is to examine children's moral development and achievement in terms of a perceived lack of legitimate parental control coupled with the opportunity to engage in peer-endorsed misbehaviour.

5

Morality and criminal justice: a first group of effects

In Peter Carey's novel *Bliss* (1981), David Joy is an adolescent searching for an emotional investment from his parents. He tells his father, 'You are head of the household. You should lead us. You should punish us.... There's no discipline, that's what's wrong.' David fails to attract his father's concern or his mother's. He turns to delinquency. A drug dealer and a thief, he winds up a victim of his dreams that some day he will become the object of his family's admiration.

Delinquency is certainly a multicausal phenomenon. As Walker has written (1977, p. 143), 'The quest for a general theory which will account for all instances of crime or deviance or misbehaviour makes no more sense than would a search for a general theory of disease'. Besides those factors influencing the person's early environment and upbringing, there are many other groups of variables which contribute to an understanding of delinquent acts. These are likely to be correlated together in complex ways (see, for example, Clarke 1978, p. 4). Nevertheless, results from a variety of studies point increasingly to children's perceptions of control as a factor of considerable importance in delinquent behaviour.

Children who are delinquent often do not come to see a clear boundary between behaviour which is controllable and under personal responsibility and that behaviour which is guided through parental or external authority. Though delinquents are more likely than non-delinquents to claim their own offences are not serious (Hindelang 1974), non-delinquents recognize circumstances for mitigating the punishment of a perpetrator. By contrast, delinquents may not recognize any justification at all for dealing with offenders in terms of the controllability of their actions. No allowance may be made for their youth or for intellectual or emotional handicaps.

In this way, many delinquents appear to languish at an objective responsibility stage similar to that originally described by Piaget in which judgements of misdeeds are based on the degree of damage caused rather than on the intentions of the perpetrator (Jurkovic 1980). Thus it is appropriate to examine the nature of mitigating circumstances, how responsibility for criminal acts is perceived by children and by adolescent offenders and non-offenders, and how responsibility is related to perceived parental competency and control.

The nature of mitigating circumstances

Though the severity of punishment is influenced by the type of situation and mental state of the criminal, mitigation requires the accused to be convicted of a crime. Mitigation is made out if 'he was exposed to an unusual or specially great temptation, or his ability to control his action is thought to have been impaired or weakened otherwise than by his own action, so that conformity to the law which he has broken was a matter of special difficulty for him as compared with normal persons normally placed' (Hart 1968, p. 15).

A diminished capacity to control events, involving the inability of an accused to form the *mens rea* of an offence owing to mental illness or mental deficit, has long been recognized in American law, and is behind the concept of degrees of homicide. In England, the defence of diminished responsibility, saying that a mentally disordered person shall not be convicted of murder if the disorder substantially impaired the perpetrator's mental responsibility, was created in 1959 by legislation. However, precisely what constitutes such 'mental disorder' varies greatly across jurisdictions and remains a matter of long-standing controversy among judges, jurors, and the general public (Tygart 1982). Indeed, there may be no legal rules of procedure for the presentation of mitigating information between when a defendant is convicted and sentenced (Shapland 1981, p. 1). *Any* information may be contained in the pleas for mitigation. What is held as valid is left to the discretion of the sentencer.

Frequently, it is up to the defendant's legal representative to discern the individual biases of the sentencer. Mental disorder by virtue of brain damage, passion, and economic condition have all been offered as mitigating circumstances associated with an inability to control events. It can be argued that none of these three conditions is 'uniquely overpowering', that the behaviour of mental disordered persons, however influenced, should not be regarded as 'totally out of control', and that such persons should, save in extreme cases, be held legally responsible for their actions (Morse 1979, p. 291). Nevertheless, the brain damage or neuropsychological defence has traditionally been allowed by courts in countries such as England and Australia, and the social psychological crime of passion defence (for example, the jilted lover overwhelmed by emotions) has often been employed in many West European jurisdictions.

Information on the economic situation of the perpetrator of a crime, while not so readily recognized as a reason to reduce or suspend criminal penalties, has often been entertained by courts. Personal economic circumstances are not uncommonly said to diminish the responsibility of the accused. In Shapland's (1981) investigation of 100 court cases, 71 out of 167 factors offered as reasons for lawbreaking dealt with personal circumstances. Moreover, recent psychological evidence, consistent with the trickle-down framework discussed in Chapter 1 of this book, points to unemployment and deprived economic conditions as antecedents of behaviour disorder and offences such as child abuse. By the same token, government bodies have often expressed the view that a link exists between crime and deprived economic conditions. For example, investigations of criminal activities apparently committed senselessly by young people during the Liverpool riots of July 1981, have identified unmet economic needs as a factor contributing to anarchy and civil unrest. This is an important point for while court verdicts may disallow economic need as a mitigating circumstance, it may still be a valid reason in the minds of many children and youths cognizant of criminal activities—leading to a breakdown in communication between the authorities and certain sections of the community.

The controversy over accepting passion and economic need as forming the basis behind an inability to control events and therefore as mitigating circumstances bears a close affinity to the debate among researchers, also discussed in Chapter 1, over the validity of non-reductionist explanations. Whilst a consensus has seemed to emerge among some researchers that the best hope for understanding aberrant human behaviour lies with work done in the neurosciences (for example, on the consequences of brain damage), others have recently attacked this view. Their claim is that non-reductionist explanations, focusing on socioeconomic conditions and social psychological phenomena such as those involving elements of passion, are at least equally viable alternatives.

In a study by Brown and Lallijee (1981), adolescents aged 15–17 years were given a questionnaire and asked to list five crimes, the appropriate punishment for each crime, and the type of circumstances under which the punishment would be reduced. The offences were placed in two categories. The first dealt with serious crimes such as murder and rape; the second pertained to less serious ones—stealing, motoring offences, drugs, breaking and entering. For most of the crimes, a variety of mitigating circumstances were provided including those relating to an inability to control events owing to brain damage, passion, or economic need as well as others involving revenge, provocation, and coercion. In cases of serious crime, insanity and mental retardation were seen as especially relevant circumstances.

Studies of the development of children's perceptions of transgressions under mitigating circumstances of provocation and coercion have indicated that even young children aged 5–6 years can mitigate the severity of their judgements in making allowances for external temptations (Berg-Cross 1975; Darley, Klosson, and Zanna 1978). Work generated from Heider's (1958) approach to moral judgement development (Fincham and Jaspars 1979; Harris 1977) suggests that young children are more likely than older ones to ascribe blame and responsibility to actors who behave in both an uncoerced and unintentional fashion corresponding to Heider's level of 'causality'. This is consistent with Piaget's (1977*b*) observation that young children may judge accidental acts more severely than their older counterparts.

Comparatively little research exists, however, that is specifically germane to perceptions of criminal justice where the perpetrator is simply said to be unable to think clearly and control events, and a similar and striking gap exists in knowledge about moral judgements of an actor's uncontrollable behaviour (Whiteman 1979).

Though subjects are able to identify a wide range of mitigating circumstances, some of which have been traditionally acceptable in a court of law, the actual degree to which subjects perceive each of these circumstances as mitigating the extent of punishment has not been determined. Moreover, since most studies have been restricted either to young children or adolescents, the question of whether there are developmental differences in the use of mitigating circumstances needs to be posed.

Mitigating circumstances in children's and juveniles' legal judgements

Two studies were designed to examine children's and juveniles' legal judgements in situations corresponding to the well-known distinctions of crimes against persons, property, and the dignity of the state (Cohn and Udolf 1979). Frequently recurring crimes falling into these three categories are assault, arson, and treason. The crimes were paired with mitigating circumstances cast in the form of an inability to control events, involving brain damage, passion, and economic need. In the first study (Irving and Siegal 1983), it was expected, following Piaget and Heider, that younger children would generally judge uncontrolled, unintentional criminal acts more severely than their older counterparts. But no specific predictions were made with regard to their evaluations of particular mitigating circumstances.

The subjects were 80 children from four grades: grade 2 (age range in years and months 6 years 7 months to 7 years 5 months, mean 7 years 1 month), grade 6 (range 10 years 7 months to 12 years, mean 11 years 3 months), grade 9 (range 13 years 7 months to 15 years, mean 14 years 2 months), and grade 12 (range 16 years 9 months to 17 years 10 months, mean 17 years 3 months). All the students received 12 stories, three of which represented the control condition and nine the experimental condition.

The stories in the control condition consisted of three crimes without mitigating circumstances. The first, assault, involved a crime against a person:

Mr A was walking down the street when he saw a person walking towards him. He went up to the person and punched him in the face. The person had a broken nose and had to be taken to hospital.

The second, arson, involved a crime against property:

Mr B saw another person's car parked by the footpath. He went over to it and set it alight with some kerosene and matches. The car was badly burned and had to be towed away.

The third, treason, involved a crime against the dignity of the state:

Mr C knew where a large amount of uranium was kept. (The younger children were told that uranium is a rock that is used to make bombs.) The place where the uranium was kept was a secret and no-one was supposed to know about it. But Mr C told some people from another country about it. This country wanted to build bombs which might be used in a war against their country.

In actual court cases, the charges are heard together with the defendant's plea prior to the presentation of any mitigating circumstances. Thus, as in the Darley, Klosson, and Zanna (1978) study, mitigating circumstances were appended to the description of the crimes. In the experimental conditions, each description was followed by one of three circumstances:

1.   Mr A didn't have a job. He had been looking for one for a long time and had spent nearly all his money. Now he did not have enough money to pay the bills and buy food and clothes for himself. He was so poor and unhappy that he was not able to think properly.
2.   Mr B's mother had died and he was very sad. All he could think about was how much he had loved her. This made him so upset that he was not able to think properly.
3.   Mr C had been in a car accident and had hit his head very hard against a door. The doctors said that he had hurt his brain and wouldn't be able to think properly.

Three sets of stories corresponding to the three crimes were presented. Within each set, three offenders were described as having committed the same crime and three different circumstances associated with mental disorders were offered as grounds for mitigating sentences.

The 7-year-olds were tested individually, and the older children in groups of five. At the outset, the children were told that they were to be given stories about some men who did some bad things and that they were to say how much punishment each man should get. The child was then shown a large white sheet of paper on which there was a large zero followed by six rectangles of increasing height and width. Each was labelled to represent the length of sentence indicated by that rectangle: 1, 5, 10, 20, 30, L (life/capital punishment).

The legal judgements of children at all ages were influenced by the type of crime. With increasing age, judgements concerning mitigating circumstances became less focused on benevolence toward individuals and more oriented to a recognition of laws as necessary dimensions of society which must not be broken for fear of disrupting the social order. Younger children may mitigate punishment on the basis of an individual's family needs or psychological state; adolescents, by contrast, focus on the importance of laws in safeguarding members of the community (Adelson, Green, and O'Neil 1969).

For the older subjects, the only consistently recognized mitigating circumstance was the case of brain damage. Economic need and passion were not generally regarded as acceptable explanations of an ability to control one's actions.

Age differences are illustrated by the subjects' explanations. For example, in justifying passion as a circumstance mitigating punishment for assault, a 7-year-old would say 'If his mother died, well he's just upset and he didn't know and wasn't thinking clearly'. By contrast, 17-year-olds would typically reject this type of mitigation plea. For example, 'if all of us who had pent up anxieties and inner depressions went around assaulting people publicly, society (law and order) would just disintegrate. But the term of punishment befits the crime; the individuals will pay sufficiently for one rash act.'

Delinquency, disordered behaviour, and perceptions of parental control

A follow-up study (Siegal 1984a) turned to a comparison of mitigating circumstances as seen by delinquent and non-delinquent adolescent boys. The subjects were 20 offenders in a government correctional facility for minors who were matched for chronological age, mental age, and socioeconomic status with a group of non-offenders drawn from a high school located adjacent to a large public housing estate. Both groups had a mean age of about $14\frac{1}{2}$ years, were of average intelligence, and had a working-class background.

The procedures was similar to that in the previous study. The major difference was that, apart from a slight change in the rating scale, the passion or social psychological circumstance was altered. The perpetrator's behaviour was said to have been associated with disordered thought processes owing to a fight with a girl friend.

The results are shown in Table 5.1 and are clear-cut. Only in the

Table 5.1 Means and standard deviations of judgements in the four conditions
(from Siegal 1984a)

		No mitigation (control)	Socioeconomic	Social-psychological	Neuropsychological
			Type of mitigating circumstance		
Offenders					
$n=20$	M	3.57	3.27	3.35	2.71
	SD	0.82	0.88	1.15	1.43
Nonoffenders					
$n=20$	M	3.95	3.48	3.40	1.70
	SD	0.83	1.01	0.98	0.70

The scale range is from 1 to 7. Higher figures represent longer sentences.

neuropsychological condition was the difference between the groups significant. Offenders judged the brain-damaged perpetrator more severely than did the non-offenders. Moreover they did not differentiate among the three conditions in which a mitigating circumstance was offered and the sole significant difference was that between the no mitigation and neuropsychological conditions. Not only did the non-offenders differentiate between these two conditions, but they also judged the socioeconomic and social psychological mitigation pleas more severely than the neuropsychological one.

The difference between the two groups on the neuropsychological condition is reflected in the subjects' justifications. These were coded into two categories: (1) that the brain-damaged perpetrator 'should be kept off the streets' or 'He'd never learn. He'd do it all the time. He needs putting away' and (2) that he 'needs help'. The criterion for placing a response in one of these categories was the strict conformity of responses, as determined by the agreement of two independent scorers, to these prototypes, the former indicating that the perpetrator should be brought in line and controlled, the latter that he should be helped to gain control himself. On average in their three judgements of the brain-damaged perpetrator, boys in the offender group would use the 'keep off the streets' justification more frequently than the 'needs help' category. By contrast, the non-offender group used either type of justification with equal frequency.

Several limitations should be stressed when considering these results. They are based on a small sample size which did not include offenders whose crime was committed in a group. Subjects were asked to give legal rather than moral judgements and thus any relation to theories of moral judgement development outside the context of judgements of sentencing and responsibility should be treated with caution. As in the previous study, the issue of culpability, which can be regarded as separate from that of sentencing, is left unaddressed. In addition, the results do not provide direct information on the relation between types of mitigation pleas and the purposes of sentencing as seen by offenders and non-offenders.

Bearing these limitations in mind, the offenders' lack of discrimination among mitigating circumstances can be seen as revealing an external orientation to rule-following partly consistent with the developmental approach of Piaget (1977*b*) and Kohlberg (1969). As in previous studies (Fodor 1972; Hudgins and Prentice 1973; Jurkovic and Prentice 1977; Nucci and Herman 1982), the present results suggest that behaviourally disordered youth are less likely to discriminate among degrees of responsibility underlying violations of the law. Rather than the law being regarded as necessary to maintain social order or as a contractual arrangement capable of adaptation to circumstance, it is seen simply as defining the wrongness of acts (Tapp and Kohlberg 1977). The offender is concerned with material consequence rather than intention and with social sanction rather than individual circumstance.

Following Janoff-Bulman and Brickman (1980), Rothbaum, Weisz, and Snyder (1982, p. 5) have proposed a two-process model of control: that 'people attempt to gain control not only by bringing the environment into line with their wishes (*primary* control) but also by bringing themselves into line with environmental forces (*secondary* control)'. The offenders' inability to differentiate among mitigating circumstances can be seen in terms of secondary control processes rather than an egocentric orientation. Instead of attempting to understand social problems so as to be actively able to solve and prevent recurrences, there is an attempt to understand problems so as to derive meaning through acceptance. There is an effort to sustain the perception of control which does not involve a clear acknowledgement of variations in individuals' abilities to master their own circumstances.

In seeking secondary control, delinquents may not view those who transgress as deserving of more autonomy but as requiring what is perceived to be authoritative firm control and intervention. In this sense the responses of juvenile offenders may be similar to those of young children, as discussed in the previous chapter. The issue for offenders may not be whether a law-breaker's actions are controllable but rather that he should have been stopped in the first place.

That delinquents are oriented toward an external control insufficient for orderly, intrinsically motivated rule-guided behaviour is shown in a study by Nucci and Herman (1982). In addition to the moral and social domain discussed in Chapter 4 of this volume, this study concerned what Nucci (1981) defines as a personal domain for which issues of right and wrong are ones of personal preference such as the nature of one's correspondence, recreational activities, and physical appearance.

The subjects were 22 normally behaved and 20 behaviourally disordered children who attended fourth grade in special education classrooms operated by two neighbouring public school districts in the west Chicago suburbs. Their mean age was about 9 years 8 months. The children were identified as behaviourally disordered through high teacher ratings for acting out behaviours such as clowning and fighting accompanied by low ratings for withdrawal and depression.

The children were presented with 15 items regarded by Nucci and Herman to be representative of those within the three domains. The five moral items concerned hitting, deception, allowing another to be punished for one's misdeed, stealing, and selfishness. Likewise, there were five social conventional items (swearing, eating with fingers, addressing teacher by the first name, being naked in public, and standing out of line) and five personal items (keeping phone calls private, watching TV on sunny days, boy wearing long hair, interacting with a forbidden friend, and eating peanut butter on baloney).

There were three phases in the procedure. First, the various items were presented in sets of three with each set containing one item from each domain. Each child was asked to order the severity of the acts from 'most wrong' to 'least wrong/not wrong' and to give explanations for their ranking. Second, the children were asked to identify the acts which would be wrong even if there was no rule. Third, they were asked to identify which of the acts should be considered the person's own business. In other words, the subjects were asked to identify acts as belonging to the moral and personal domains.

While normal and behaviourally disordered children did not differ in their rankings, their explanations did differ. Normals were more likely to give explanations centring on the personal consequences of acts to the person involved and on the retribution of peers victimized by the act. By contrast, behaviourally disordered children focused on the sheer absurdity or injustice of acts and on acts as resulting in punishment by adult authorities.

The two groups also differed in their choices of items as moral and personal. Only 11 of the 20 behaviourally disordered children indicated that hitting would be wrong in the absence of a rule compared with 21 out of 22 normals. The behaviourally disordered also identified fewer personal acts as within the realm of the person's own business. For example, only a chance level of 11 out of 20 indicated that to watch TV on a sunny day should be the person's own business as opposed to 19 of the normals

When compared with normals, behaviourally disordered children seem likely to identify fewer acts as moral, orient more toward adults and less to peer reactions as a basis for identifying the wrongness of moral acts, and are reluctant to identify acts as within the personal domain. They seem less certain of the bounds of individual and societal realms of authority, the latter tending to overwhelm the former. As Nucci and Herman suggest, such children do not appear to possess a sense of 'personal autonomy'.

A lack of autonomy is associated with perceptions of parents as failing to meet the obligations of parenthood, particularly those involving 'caring' or 'concerned supervision'. Delinquents' legal and moral judgements may not be determinants of their actions but *post hoc* rationalizations of disordered behaviour determined by a lack of perceived parental control. In an Australian study (Kraus 1977), delinquents in an institution and boys from a high delinquency area in Sydney were asked to indicate what they regarded as the common causes of offending. Peer influences, thrill-seeking, boredom, or material or monetary gain were often mentioned. But most frequently, parental inadequacy was cited in the form of a bad home life, broken home, and cruel or neglectful parents. Wilson (1980) in fact claims that parental supervision has been overlooked in delinquency research. In her study, families from the English West Midlands were divided equally into six groups of 20 according to the parents' social handicap (classified as low, moderate, or severe, according to a scoring system recording social class, family size, adequacy of school clothing, school attendance and parental contact with school) and residential area (inner city or suburban). Neither hardship nor area of residence were as strong a predictor of sons' delinquency as were parents' self-reports of permissive child-rearing behaviour.

No attempt was made in either the Kraus or the Wilson studies to control for extraneous factors such as parental intelligence which may have accounted for the permissive upbringing. Yet the pattern of results is broadly similar to the American studies of McCord (1979) and others discussed in Chapter 1 of this volume. Moreover, the work of Patterson (1981) which has involved observations of family interactions points to unclear rules, a lack of differentiation among situations, and the absence of a non-critical parental interest as factors which contribute to children's problem behaviour. An extensive review by Loeber and Dishion (1983) indicates that composite measures of family management techniques tend to be most predictive of male delinquency. Altogether, the evidence suggests that a perceived lack of control underlying parents' childrearing techniques plays a considerable role.

These perceptions may discriminate delinquents who act out when receiving residential treatment from those who respond. Richman and Harper (1979) took 54 male adolescents with a mean age of 15 years and mean IQ of 94. They were referred by a court in

Iowa for a 20-day evaluation and treatment programme geared for delinquents who are 'usually too difficult to manage in the family, yet not severe enough to warrant closed institutional placement'. The boys indicated their parents' patterns of childrearing techniques on the Child Report of Parental Behavior Inventory (Schaefer 1965*a* and *b*). Those boys who were rated as maintaining a high level of acting out during treatment were more likely to perceive their mothers as lax in control and accepting of their behaviour than those who responded favourably in exhibiting increased self-control.

Control, delinquency and opportunity

To this analysis a qualification must be added. Despite the nature of the home environment, at minimum the opportunity has to exist before children can actually engage in delinquent acts. Opportunity may be provided through leisure time spent on the streets which can exert an effect on children's behavioural control independently of their perceptions of parental inadequacy. Exposure to non-parental and particularly peer-group influences can affect children's willingness to comply with adult rules and standards for behaviour.

Two recent studies, one in Britain (Gladstone 1978) and the other in Holland (Van Dijk and Steinmetz 1982), have underscored the cumulative effects of unsatisfactory parent–child relations and leisure time. The British subjects were 584 boys aged 11–15 years attending maintained secondary schools in a city in the north of England. The Dutch study examined the self-reports of 1825 boys living in two cities. The English boys were asked anonymously to report on their involvement in vandalism, the average number of hours spent on the street each evening, and their parents' attitude to 'hanging around the streets'. Similarly, the Dutch boys were asked to report on their delinquent acts, the extensiveness of their leisure time, and their truancy or running away from home.

The results are shown in Tables 5.2 and 5.3: 53 per cent of English boys without strict parents spending 3 hours or more on the street reported engaging in a high degree of vandalism; among Dutch boys reporting both extensive leisure time and truancy or running away, 79 per cent reported committing delinquent acts. Comparable percentages for boys not reporting these two characteristics were 11 and 30 respectively.

Van Dijk and Steinmetz (1982) suggest that, in spite of the perceived or actual control imposed by parents, children can be enticed

Table 5.2 Percentages of English boys reporting involvement in vandalism
(from Gladstone 1978, p. 28)

	Hours spent on street		Self-reported involvement	*n*
No perceived strict parental attitude to 'hanging around the streets'	3 or more	high	53	92
		medium	37	64
		low	11	19
	less than 3	high	41	53
		medium	30	39
		low	29	37
Perceived strict parental attitude	3 or more	high	47	42
		medium	36	32
		low	18	16
	less than 3	high	11	21
		medium	32	61
		low	57	108
				584

Table 5.3 Percentages of Dutch boys reporting involvement in crime
(from Van Dijk and Steinmitz 1982)

	Leisure time	Self-reported crimes (one or more)	*n*
Truancy/ Running away from home	extensive	79	148
	average	62	209
	little	55	100
No truancy/ running away	extensive	51	292
	average	39	620
	little	30	456
			1825

to offend during their free time. It is then that they are exposed to potential offenders and become susceptible to victimization from others. Children react by becoming offenders themselves. For example, having one's own bicycle stolen can contribute to a propensity toward committing acts of theft.

Research is needed to examine the quality of adolescent free time. No doubt the pursuit of 'leisure' can be less stressful in prosperous times than in times of economic deprivation. Undesirable changes in socioeconomic conditions and consequent victimization can change children's belief in the moral rightness of a rule against stealing. In this context, stealing may become regarded as a ritual or personal matter, or even a social convention which justifies its permissibility. As Rutter and Giller (1983, pp. 248–50, 265) remark, when viewed in the context of perceived parental inadequacy, peer-group influence may have 'more substance' as an explanation for delinquency than was once supposed. Again, Baldwin's maxim that children practise in the peer group what they learn from adults is certainly relevant. Elements of delinquent behaviour can reflect the combination of a perceived lack of parental control and a victimization by peers during free time.

6

Achievement and economic justice:
a second group of effects

Investigations into the relation between achievement, economic justice, and social development have come from two sources. One concerns how children and adolescents perceive adult economic arrangements and the world of work; the other involves the effectiveness of mothers and fathers as parents in terms of roles played within the family. Research in both areas has mushroomed with little connection between the two.

No doubt this isolation can be partly seen in terms of a focus on microsystem characteristics to the exclusion of those in the mesosystem and exosystem, and vice versa. With regard to the microsystem, the world of family and domestic needs has traditionally been under the aegis of the mother. With regard to the mesosystem and exosystem, the world of work and issues of effort, ability, and productivity remains predominantly masculine. The worlds of work and family in industrial Western society have for the most part been studied separately, and investigators have been inclined to treat each world as self-contained in its own right.

To bridge the two areas of study is no easy matter. Any attempt at integration will necessarily be fraught with speculation, but it can be conjectured that, within the context of the 'traditional family', children perceive the father's success as an economic achiever and provider to constitute a measure of his effectiveness as a parent. Conversely, the mother's effectiveness is influenced by children's perceptions of her activities inside and outside of the family. Thus children's concern for family needs may to a considerable extent be based on favourable perceptions of the mother; at the same time, their achievement, their orientations toward the world of work and the distribution of resources among workers may be based on favourable perceptions of fathers.

In the traditional family, the mother and father play complementary roles. The mother provides for emotional needs by creating and maintaining family solidarity. Her expressive leadership is in contrast with the instrumental leadership shown by the father in providing for economic needs and dealing with the world of work. As Sagi (1982, p. 206) points out, this typology has often been used to distinguish traditional from non-traditional families and originates from Parsons and Bales (1955). Though the expressive-instrumental distinction may often be unclear in contemporary Western families (Maccoby and Jacklin 1974, p. 262), the notion of a traditional family still serves to illuminate the development of achievement and economic justice in many instances. Changes in the nature of the traditional family which have led to non-traditional arrangements such as in the two-income, one-parent, or father-caregiver family will be taken up in Chapter 8 of this volume.

Theories of socialization in the traditional family still require more scrutiny before firm conclusions can be drawn. However, with the increase in cross-cultural studies and in studies which have examined the decision-making impact of the father, a number of tentative findings have begun to emerge. First, the relationship between children's perceptions of economic roles and the effectiveness of mothers and fathers as parents will be examined. Then Western adolescents' perceptions of economic and family roles will be compared to those of Japanese adolescents who are immersed in an industrial culture in which the worlds of work and family are more fully integrated.

Children's perceptions of adult economic arrangements and responsibilities

Considerable attention has been devoted to the study of children's understanding of economic arrangements. Children's perceptions of the differences between rich and poor have been examined, and descriptions and evaluations elicited, in studies conducted in Australia (Connell 1970), Canada (Baldus and Tribe 1978; Siegal 1981), Britain (Furth, Baur, and Smith 1976; G. Jahoda 1979), and the United States (Leahy 1983). These have indicated that children of all ages are not always sensitive to, or even aware of, the plight of the economically deprived, and that their perceptions of adult needs can first be characterized by an undifferentiated understanding of different roles and occupations which gradually gives way to a recognition of inequalities. During adolescence, there emerges an understanding of concepts of social structure; fairness and the balance of rights among individuals comes to be viewed in terms of viability of political and economic institutions (Turiel 1983a, pp. 102–12).

Leahy's work provides one example. The participants, aged 6–17 years, were enrolled in schools located in the Boston, New York, and Washington, DC metropolitan areas. They came from a mixture of middle- and working-class backgrounds. All subjects were interviewed to elicit descriptions and evaluations of differences between rich and poor. The younger children generally believed that adults are motivated out of benevolence. While young children often did not recognize the existence of poverty, older children predominantly believed that poverty is the person's own responsibility. As in previous studies (Connell 1970), descriptions and comparisons of the rich and the poor were generally unrelated to social class. Justifications of inequality were associated with increasing age, perhaps fuelled by the subjects' belief that they themselves could become rich some day if they so desired.

Interview studies, however, have their drawbacks, not the least of which is that respondents can be influenced by the characteristics of the interviewer. But the interview results are in line with experimental evidence that children in Western countries are often insensitive or at least unaware of the plight of those in difficult economic circumstances. In a study by Weiner and Peter (1973), the subjects were aged 4–18 years and were drawn from daycare centres and schools located in lower middle-class districts of Los Angeles. They were asked to evaluate story situations in which a child worked at a puzzle task and was described according to the eight possible combinations of effort (high or low), ability (present or absent), and outcome (successful or unsuccessful completion of the puzzle). Up until the age of 12 years, the level of effort replaced outcome as the primary determinant of achievement evaluations. But during adolescence, outcome again became the most important factor. The interpretation of these findings is that society reinforces the re-emergence of outcome as a developmental stage, and that such is particularly the case in industrial Western society (Salili, Maehr, and Gillmore 1976).

The orientations of adolescents towards the unemployed provides some additional support for a social reinforcement explanation. In an Australian study (Ho and Smithson 1981), three groups (high school students, unemployed persons, and employed persons), matched for age, sex, and education level, were given a questionnaire to identify causal attributions for unemployment and employment status. They rated six internal/dispositional attributions items and nine external/socioenvironmental items on a four-point scale: true for most, true for some, true for few, and true for none. The internal items consisted of statements such as 'The unemployed are lazy and they don't try hard enough for work'. High ratings were given to these statements by the employed and school leaver groups in contrast to the unemployed group who preferred to give external attributions such as 'The government is trying to reduce inflation at the expense of the unemployed' and 'Employers are not willing to sacrifice profits to create jobs'.

Similar results have come from an Australian longitudinal study (Gurney 1981). Moreover, the intensive cross-sectional studies of Furnham (1982*a* and *b*) in England indicate that the internal or individualistic explanations which adults give for unemployment and poverty in Britain have greater support among the less educated than the more highly educated and, not unsurprisingly, among Conservative rather than Labour voters.

The acceptability of internal explanations in Britain appears to be greater than in other European countries (Brown and Madge 1982, pp. 179–80). As Scarse (1974) points out in a comparative study of English and Swedish workers, perceptions of external causes for deprivation and feelings of victimization depend on a point of reference. Should the deprived compare themselves with other deprived, such causes are not salient. Swedish workers are more likely than their English counterparts to widen their focus in comparing themselves to non-deprived white-collar workers; they ascribe to more external explanations for deprivation relating to the structural inequality of society.

Three concepts of fairness

Curiously, there are many other studies in which it has been presumed that a fair distribution of economic rewards can indeed take place without considering the needs of individuals in a socioeconomic context. Scores of studies, mostly carried out in the United States, have been generated by equity theory: that one's rewards should be divided on the principle that reward allocations or outcomes should correspond to the relevant contributions (inputs) of individuals (Adams 1965).

While adults are said to abide by the equity norm, younger children appear to adopt an allocation strategy of equality, that is dividing rewards equally among workers regardless of their contributions. For example, Nelson and Dweck (1977) examined the use of equity in young children by having preschoolers work on a task with another child or as 'supervisors' for two other fictitious child workers. Only when the experimenter made the 'social demand' for equity explicit did child supervisors without self-interest use the equity principle. Otherwise, the equality strategy was employed.

Hook and Cook (1979) in a comprehensive review of the research are able to make a strong case that our ability to use the equity principle is largely a function of cognitive development. Other studies have extended equity research to judgements of allocations for damage and have made reference to social norms as well as to cognitive development. But these also have not included an examination of need.

The concept of fairness as indicative of need is inherently social and must relate to social factors. Still, these might not be seen as socioeconomic ones. There are studies which propose that this type of fairness proceeds from an egocentric orientation to one in which there is a belief in distributing wealth according to need. Damon (1975) has proposed a sequence of distributive justice along these lines:

Stage

0-A The child believes that whoever wants the most money on goods should have it.

0-B The child bases distributive decisions on external characteristics; the tallest or oldest one, for example, should get more than the others.

1-A The child believes everyone should receive the same amount regardless of other characteristics.

1-B The child bases distributive decisions on behavioural reciprocity; there is a belief that those who work harder or do more than the others should get more.

2-A The child bases distributive decisions on psychological reciprocity; that is, the child believes that those who are most in need should receive more than the others.

An example of research based on Damon's sequence comes from a study by Enright, Enright, and Lapsley (1981). Kindergarten children and third-grade children of lower-class and middle-class families in southern Florida were given a distributive justice scale consisting of two dilemmas. They were asked to respond by choosing a picture which corresponded to one of Damon's stages. For instance, in one dilemma, four children are said to be in the same classroom and their teacher lets them make paintings which they sell. The subjects had to decide how to split up 5 cent pieces among children with the following characteristics: Sue who wants the money more than the others (Stage 0-A); Jim who is the biggest (0-B); Mary who has made the most pictures (1-B); and Billy who comes from a poor family (2-A). There is also a 1-A example in which the experimenter says, 'In this picture, all children get the same number of nickels so there won't be any fights about who gets more'.

The progression, then, is to assume to represent a development of fairness in children toward a preference for the 2-A or need alternative. Using this procedure the predicted age and social class differences are found with older and middle-class children embracing higher stages more than younger and working-class ones. These findings held even when verbal intelligence was partialled out.

Enright, Enright, and Lapsley (1981) claim that peer-group socialization may influence the children's allocations since small but insignificant correlations emerged between being judged as fair and likeable by one's classmates and responses on the distributive justice measure. These were of the order of 0.25 and 0.28. However, several points must be made about this type of study. First, it is unlikely that young children can be regarded as egocentric and as simply wanting more. Second, family income, and not a gross measure of social class, might have been a better predictor of allocations. Third, distributive justice as a function of social class may importantly reflect the home and school environment. Working-class children may be less likely to learn that giving to the poor is an acceptable social convention or moral rule.

In Western society, there are many cases in which cooperation declines with age and competition increases (Siegal 1982, pp. 64–6). The concept of fairness can transcend conventional norms to apply universally. Issues of fairness do arise in the microsystem of relations between equals such as two adults or two children where no other dependent persons are involved. They also arise in the mesosystem of relations which encompass children indirectly such as those bodies which liaise between families and schools. But these matters must be seen in their proper perspective within a socioeconomic context.

Even though fairness in the first two senses may increase during childhood, a concern for fairness in the exosystem, for the needs of economically deprived individuals, may actually decline during adolescence. To illustrate from Turiel's (1983a) standpoint, it may be a social convention in school to reward a poor child with an extra 5 cents. By contrast, there may be a universal moral rule observed by many not to give an extra $10 to family welfare agencies out of a fear that recipients will lose the incentive to work. Fairness may also be selective in individuals' willingness to compensate the financial needs of relatives while at the same time disregarding the needs of the economically deprived in general.

Thus one of the core elements in fairness resides squarely in the individual's appraisal of institutions within the exosystem, and of political and economic policies designed to provide for family economic needs. The antecedents of fairness in each of these three senses are probably quite different. Fairness in the microsystem and mesosystem contexts is influenced by cognitive development as well as an understanding of social conventions. Fairness in the exosystem context is a matter involving children's perceptions of important others which contributes to their self-definition. In many cases, a 'cool' cognitive development characterized by a sequence of stages may play an insignificant role.

Mothers, fathers, and children's concern for need in a socioeconomic context

If a concern with others' economic needs may diminish during adolescence, does this decline reflect a male individual ethos in adolescents' perceptions of economic arrangements? Hoffman (1977) has shown that studies on empathy, when considered as a whole, indicate a small but significant tendency for females to be more empathic than males and for children's concern for others to be related to their parents' self-reports of holding altruistic values. According to Hoffman (1975), the pressure to achieve and succeed in males may often conflict with a concern for the welfare of others. In the process of socialization, boys come to resemble their fathers and fit into the traditional 'instrumental' sex-role geared toward occupational success and achievement. But what if boys express a desire to be like their mothers instead of their fathers? Might they then relinquish a belief in the 'equal pay for equal work' norm in favour of a norm which prescribes that resources ought to be allocated according to family needs?

These questions were addressed in a recent study (Winocur and Siegal 1982). Two age groups of middle-class Australian adolescents aged 12–13 and 16–18 years were given Hoffman's (1971) self-report measure of identification. They also were asked to allocate rewards between a fictitious male and female worker in four separate cases. In one case, a male with no children was contrasted with a female with three children. In a second, a male with three children was contrasted with a female who had none. In the third and fourth cases, both workers had no children and both had two children respectively.

For each of the cases, subjects were asked to divide a pile of 12 A$50 notes from the game 'Monopoly' between the two workers. The total figure of $600 was chosen so that, if the money was divided equally, each worker would receive $50 above the average industrial male wage which was $250 at the time.

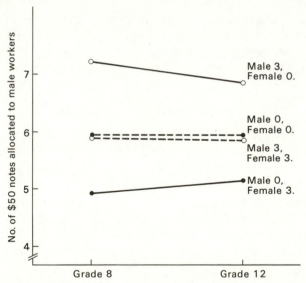

Fig. 6.1.   Reward allocations in the four conditions (Winocur and Siegal 1982).

As expected, concern for need declined with age (Fig. 6.1). Older adolescents were more likely than younger ones to base their allocations on a norm for equal work for equal pay, ignoring the family needs of individual workers. Moreover, boys' concern for need was correlated with mother identification, suggesting that the female is a source of empathy incompatible with the individual male ethos upon which the equal pay for equal work norm is based.

To a not inconsiderable extent individual economic success in Western countries may be based on this ethos. McClelland (1975;

McClelland and Pilon 1983) maintains that if the father is judged as the primary agent in his son's childrearing the boy will be more likely to show evidence of an 'imperial power syndrome', a high need to achieve and a comparatively low need for affiliation with others, coupled with a high inhibition of activity, self-control, and discipline.

This motivational pattern has been associated with managerial success. According to McClelland (1975, p. 294), it clearly relates also to a belief in a just world that the successful deserve their rewards and the needy deserve their misfortunes (Heider 1958; Lerner 1970).

Boys and girls with fathers possessing masculine attributes rather than androgynous, undifferentiated, or feminine ones as determined on the Bem Sex-Role Inventory (Bem 1974) are more likely to be judged cognitively and socially 'competent' by adult observers. According to a study by Baumrind (1982, p. 68), 'their fathers are firm, demanding, and positively reinforcing, but leave the direction of day-to-day activities to their wives; mothers are loving, responsive, and involved in supervising the activities of their children'. In this regard, McClelland (1975, p. 291) found a significant relationship between the imperial motivational pattern in men and a self-reported dislike of childcare and enjoyment of work. This evidence amounts to support for the position discussed in Chapter 2 that males are oriented toward a morality of separateness and individual rights and rules whereas females are oriented toward a morality of interdependence. It points to the possibility of gender differences in conceptions of moral rules and social conventions (Smetana 1984).

In the traditional family, perceived attributes of the remote but powerful father may entice children to achieve. According to Tesser's (1980, p. 88) analysis, when the father's achievements are perceived as very good and are relevant to the son's self-definition, comparison processes will occur. High levels of closeness will be more threatening to self-esteem than low levels and the son will be motivated to decrease closeness. Biographical information on eminent scientists and their fathers indicates that the closeness of their personal relationships was inversely related to similarity in their occupations.

Consequently, boys who are oriented toward serious academic and economic success perceive their fathers to possess forceful masculine qualities consistent with the male image of the world of work. If this type of 'ideal' father were asked for a self-description, he might deliver his reply in Shakespearean terms:

My presence, like a robe pontifical
Ne'er seen but wondered at: and so my state,
Seldom but sumptuous, show'd like a feast,
And won by rareness such solemnity.
King Henry IV Part I, III, 2

Integration of the world of work and family need: the case of Japan

In Western society, individual academic and economic achievement is not necessarily compatible with a concern for the economically deprived. The Japanese case is different in some respects. It can be used to illustrate an example of an industrial society where the worlds of work and family are more integrated (Siegal 1982, pp. 166–71).

For instance, Japanese economic arrangements are very different from those in other industrialized countries, and we might expect differences between Japanese and Western adolescents' evaluations of economic needs. Lifetime company employment is not uncommon in Japan with promotion based on seniority and there is a paternalistic relationship between superior and subordinate and between employer and employee (Hsu 1975). The rights and duties of this relationship are extended to the employee's family (Rohlen 1974). In return for employee loyalty, the company provides housing, medical insurance and treatment, and recreation. That Japanese companies treat their employees as part of a large family may be one reason for recent Japanese economic success (Cole 1979; Holden 1980; Odagiri 1982).

As Macarov (1982, p. 146) has observed, Japanese industrial relations rest on reciprocal *obligations* between employers and employees while relations in Western industrialized countries such as the United States, Britain, and Australia, rest on the *rights* of employers and employees within the work setting. A frequent Western theme is that the interests of the two are opposed with conflict between the economic viability of companies and the financial welfare and advancement of workers. In Australia, for example, industrial disputes between the parties often can only be resolved through the offices of a government arbitration commission (Connell 1977). By contrast, the Japanese workplace is characterized by a collective orientation where management caters to the personal needs of workers (Sasaki 1981). The actual salary allowance given by some Japanese firms for family support may not be of large financial importance (Tsurumi 1978, pp. 90–1). But in relation to the reward allocations of older adolescents, the family allowance given to younger men on marriage and the birth of children may be particularly salient. For young workers, unlike the old, it can represent a considerable increment in their salaries (Rohlen 1974, p. 160).

The following study (Siegal and Shwalb, in press) compared Japanese and Australian adolescents' allocations of economic rewards. In terms of the variation among Western countries in adolescents' political and economic socialization (Gallatin 1980, pp. 353–63), a Japanese–Australian comparison appears particularly appropriate. Japan and Australia have an almost identical gross national product per capita (*World Development Report*, 1982), and the two countries virtually tied for 15th place among those surveyed. Thus Australia is the closest Western equivalent to Japan in terms of per capita GNP, though this should be regarded as only a rough measure of economic performance.

A key issue in this study was the conditions of ability, effort, and work outcome under which high family need would be judged as worthy of compensation. In Japan, students in the 12–15-year-old range are not well versed in monetary matters by their parents and are not allowed to have part-time jobs with the exception of newspaper delivery. For Japanese boys, spending money ordinarily comes from cash gifts on special occasions and allowances from parents and is not tied to worker attributes. Thus with increasing age Japanese boys should become more discriminating in their allocation of rewards. Given greater familiarity with inequality and with what are adult company experiences, their concern for need should increase. Specifically, in line with the paternalistic work ethic, which is present in Japan in comparison to Western countries, it was predicted that with age Japanese adolescents would allocate more based on family need than their Australian counterparts, particularly in a situation of high economic performance as employer–employee obligations are then fulfilled.

The Australian subjects were 16 boys each at two age levels. The ages of the younger group ranged from 12 years 3 months to 13 years (mean = 12 years 6 months). The older boys ranged from 15 years 7 months to 17 years 9 months (mean = 16 years 8 months). All were Caucasian native speakers of English and attended schools in middle-class suburbs of Brisbane.

The two groups of 16 Japanese boys each were comparable in age to the Australian sample. Ages of younger boys ranged from 12 years 2 months to 13 years 2 months (mean = 12 years 8 months). The older group ranged in age from 16 years 4 months to 17 years 2 months (mean = 16 years 9 months). All attended school in middle-class suburbs of Tokyo. These two age levels represent those of students in the early and late stages of their secondary school years.

Both Japanese and Australian subjects were seen individually by a local female experimenter. As in the Winocur and Siegal (1982) study, Australian subjects were shown a large pile of imitation $50 notes from the game 'Monopoly'. In Japan, a survey of 40 pupils at another secondary school indicated that a majority of pupils felt more comfortable using two denominations of notes for allocations, rather than one. Therefore Japanese subjects were shown two piles, of 10 000 yen and 5000 yen imitation notes, worth A$40 and A$20 respectively. The other instructions and stimuli used in the Australian setting were translated into Japanese by back-translation procedures (Brislin 1980), and were identical for both cultures. The experimenter then gave pupils the following instructions:

I am going to read you descriptions of 16 workers. All have graduated from the same schools and have worked for one company for the same length of time. Some workers work hard, others do not work hard. Some know how to do their job well, others do not know how to do their job well. Some actually do their job well, others do not do their job well. Some have three children to take care of, others have no children to take care of. I want you to take this money and show me how much each of the workers should have each week to spend.

Subjects were then given the 16 descriptions of male workers in randomized order representing all possible combinations of the four evaluative dimensions—effort, ability, outcome, and need. Two examples of descriptions are as follows:

A man works hard, knows how to do his job well, does his job well, and has three children to take care of (high effort, high ability, high outcome, high family need).

A man does not work hard. Though he knows how to do his job well, he does not do it well. He has three children to take care of (low effort, high ability, low outcome, high need).

To control for possible recency effects in memory, the four pieces of information were randomized within each description. After each description was read, the subjects allocated the play money representing the weekly income for that worker.

The Australian subjects were tested in March and April of 1981 and the Japanese subjects about 1 year later. To equate for scale values, the Japanese responses in yen were converted into Australian dollars at the exchange rate when they were tested (A$1 = 255 yen), and these values were deflated by an additional 10 per cent to account for inflation between 1981 and 1982. The figures were finally divided by 50 and represented cross-culturally comparable units worth one A$50 note each. Reliability of the 16 ratings was calculated using the analyses of variance procedure for internal consistency (Winer 1970, pp. 124–8). The reliability coefficients for the younger and older Japanese subjects were 0.93 and 0.79 respectively; figures for the two Japanese age groups were 0.69 and 0.68 respectively.

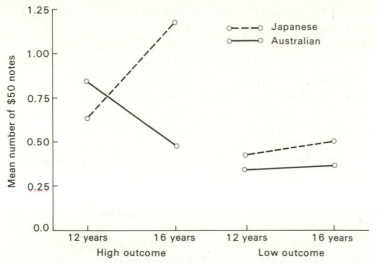

Fig. 6.2. Additional increments allocated to high need in conditions of high and low economic outcomes (from Siegal and Shwalb in press).

The main findings are shown in Fig. 6.2. As anticipated, older Japanese adolescents were most willing to reward for need when outcome was high despite effort and ability. This pattern was not significantly evident in the Australian sample. Compared to their Australian counterparts, older Japanese adolescents allocated over double the increment for high over low need when outcome was also high: A$59.50 as against A$24. These results are consistent with the Japanese practice of allocating bonuses for family need on the basis of successful outcomes. They reflect differences in philosophies of economic justice between Japan and other industrialized countries. As Sasaki (1981, pp. 6–7) remarks,

Plant managers and supervisors concern themselves with the private affairs of their workers or subordinates. Frequently, managers invite their staff for a drink after work, and it is not rare when a manager is transferred to another plant or office that his workers and subordinates come to the house to help with packing, cleaning, and other activities, and on the day he leaves they line up at the railway station to see him off. Such a scene would not be understood in Western society. What may be considered as an invasion of privacy in the West is accepted in Japan as consideration for subordinates.

In contrast to Japan, management in many Western countries assumes that work and family issues are to be considered separately as independent entities (Gutek, Namamura, and Nieva 1981; Whitehill and Takezawa 1968).

In Japan, close family relationships are thought to serve as a prototype for identification and loyalty concerning one's workplace (Caudill 1973). Further, feelings of guilt toward beneficient parents have been found as an important root of Japanese achievement motivation (DeVos 1973). The phenomenon of 'groupism' has been directly linked to success on the production floor as companies contribute to family needs (Kiefer 1970). While Japanese mothers use different childrearing strategies than their Western counterparts in that they use more 'feeling-oriented appeals' (Conroy *et al.* 1980), precisely how maternal socialization behaviour relates to workers' economic performance is unclear and merits attention.

More research is necessary to explore the relationship of parent–child relations and children's perceptions of economic arrangements and inequality as they reflect cultural norms and values as well as the rights and duties of parents and children in the family. When taken as a whole, evidence suggests that academic and economic achievement is promoted in the context of family experiences. A strong forceful image of parents, particularly the father, may be conducive to success.

Achievement and economic justice in the Western and Japanese adolescents can be seen to reflect different socialization experiences. Western children perceive the pursuit of individualism as a pathway to successful economic performance; often the world of the family is regarded as a separate issue. In Japan, company policies are geared to integrate the two worlds of work and family by providing for family needs. It should be noted, however, that Japanese workers may pay a price for the paternal work ethic. As indicated in a comprehensive review of the cross-cultural research on stress (Lynn 1982), Japanese workers report far higher stress at work than do workers in virtually every Western country.

7

Agreement, conflict, and control

Cognitive-developmental stage theorists have insisted that conflict is an important force underlying development. According to Inhelder, Sinclair, and Bovet (1974, pp. 258–9), the 'dynamic processes of progress' are characterized by cognitive 'disequilibria' which are experienced as conflicts or contradictions. Piaget (1977a, p. 39), in commenting upon the Inhelder, Sinclair, and Bovet work, stated, 'These authors showed that the most fruitful factors in the acquisition of understanding were the results of disturbances producing conflicting situations'. For Perret-Clermont (1980, p. 162),

A situation of social interaction provides not only the opportunity to initiate another child, and thereby the possibility of conflict with one's own way of doing things, but also and more often, the opportunity to elaborate actions with another child, and thus to coordinate interactions even though these may initially be different. . . . The child is then obliged, here and now, to compare self and other, and to effect a restructuring which will integrate the diverging positions. The notion of conflict holds a central place in this theoretical perspective on development; cognitive conflict created by social interactions is the locus at which the power during intellectual development is generated.

Another more interpersonal type of conflict which is proposed to stimulate development is that between the child and the parent. For Piaget (1977b), the young child's perceptions of the adult are an obstacle rather than a stimulus to development. That adult rules are to be obeyed at all costs conflicts with the more mature orientation that punishment and rule enforcement should reflect the intentions of the rule-breaker. Peer-group interaction together with the experience of being unfairly dealt with by an adult for accidentally caused damage produces the conflict between unilateral respect for the adult and a 'mutual respect' among peers which takes into account others' interests and intentions. Again, conflict will only be resolved when children relinquish an egocentric orientation and can coordinate the viewpoints of others with their own. For stage theorists, then, 'The problem of moral change would appear to be one of presenting stimuli which are both sufficiently incongruous as to stimulate conflict in the child's existing stage schemata and sufficiently congruous to be assimilable with some accommodative effort' (Kohlberg 1969, p. 402).

Agreement versus conflict

However, as seen in Chapter 4, to characterize children's early knowledge of others as broadly 'egocentric' does not do justice to their development. Apart from the issue of whether many young children can consciously verbalize the role of the other, it is abundantly clear that they can identify moral actions from non-moral ones, can discriminate emotional states, and can recognize the intentions underlying childrearing techniques. Moreover, evidence suggests that development is a product of agreement rather than conflict.

For example, in one study (P. E. Bryant 1982), it was argued that conflict tells the child that something is wrong but not what is wrong. But if two strategies produce the same answer, the child can be sure that both are right. The children in this series of experiments were six-year-olds. They were asked to measure the height of wooden blocks using direct comparisons from different levels, direct comparisons when the blocks are side by side, and indirect comparisons using a rod as a measure. Only when the two latter strategies coincided was there a significant increase in correct judgements of height.

A second study dealt with a form of cognitive conflict arising from social interaction (J. Russell 1981). Children aged 5–8 years of age attending schools in Liverpool were presented with a 'class inclusion' problem. Some children worked in pairs and were shown three green and three yellow pencils. One child was told to pick 'more pencils altogether than the partner' while the partner was instructed to pick up 'more yellow pencils' than the first child. The remaining children worked alone. They were shown a model policeman and a model fireman with a set of three yellow and three green bricks and were instructed to give 'more bricks altogether to the fireman and more yellow bricks to the policeman'.

According to the neo-Piagetian conflict hypothesis (see, for example, Perret-Clermont 1980), children working in pairs should outperform those working alone because dyads are exposed to conflicting points of view and have the opportunity to coordinate their different perspectives cooperatively. However, the two groups of children did not differ in performance. When social interaction did succeed it seemed largely due to one partner criticizing the other, forcibly taking a pencil away from the other or preventing the partner from taking an additional pencil. This would indicate a lack of cooperative acknowledgement of the different points of view. A correct solution instead appeared to stem from the incorrect partner complying with a dominant other.

Neither the Bryant nor the Russell studies are totally conclusive. In the former, children succeeded on only half of the post-test trials, indicating either that a significant number of children were not motivated to succeed by the agreement of two strategies or that for all children measurement in general remained a haphazard affair, albeit a significant improvement, on previous attempts. In the Russell study, children might not have deferred through compliance to the judgements of the correct partner but out of some more general system of cooperative social relations. A child might defer to a partner on the class inclusion problem. The partner then reciprocates by deferring to the child in another situation.

A study conducted by Damon and Killen (1982) throws some light on this question. Children aged 5–9 years were videotaped in discussions of a distributive justice problem. The children were asked to split up rewards according to the Damon positive justice technique described in Chapter 6 of this volume. Responses were scored in terms of stage responses toward an increasing recognition of fairness toward others. Contrary to the hypothesis that socio-cognitive conflict should induce advances in children's moral development, conflict worked against change. Children who disagreed, contradicted, or proposed solutions opposed to those of their peers were less likely to advance.

Evidence on the issue of conflict and agreement is in underabundant proportion to theory. All the same, these studies, together with the wealth of research on the relation between children's behaviour and their favourable perceptions of parents (involving a third form of agreement which is social and possibly more general), are certainly inconsistent with the conflict hypothesis.

Langer (1969, p. 39) has equated conflict with 'perturbation' and in the Piagetian tradition has claimed that 'the pedagogical problem, of course, is to find the right type of perturbation for each developmental stage, so that adequate rates of progress will be obtained'.

Yet Langer, as well as Perret-Clermont, have at times shown misgivings. Langer (1969, p. 34) has conceded that some children are overtly distressed and confused when presented with a conflict. Their judgements remain the same as before. Perret-Clermont (1980, pp. 141 and 161) acknowledges the possibility that an 'emotional' conflict between persons exchanging information may preclude development. If egocentrism in an inaccurate characterization of early social development and the 'self' is defined in relation to perceptions of others, it makes good sense to look for ways of improving understanding through agreement rather than conflict.

Perceptions of parental roles and emotions

Recently, much research has dealt with children's ideas about parent–child relations. Results have been interpreted to suggest that the child progresses through developmental stages in disassociating the self from perceptions of others and in representing the positions of family members in a system of kinship relations.

Watson and Amgott-Kwan (1983) used dolls to depict typical family roles about which questions were asked of children aged 3–$7\frac{1}{2}$ years. The younger children (3–$4\frac{1}{2}$ years) viewed parental roles as a 'single representation'; they could name two appropriate parental activities that do not contradict each other or apply to all humans. By 6 years of age, children have achieved a 'representational mapping' that a person can be both a father and a child of his own father; and by 7 years, they have achieved a 'representational system', for example, the notion that a father can be a son at the same time that he is a father and a grandfather.

In this way, the child comes to reflect on the role of a child in a parent–child relationship. Cognitive-developmental theorists have sought to identify stages in the child's perception of the obligations of parenthood in relation to those of childhood. Working independently, Damon (1977, pp. 178–9), Harter (1982a; Harter and Barnes 1981), and Selman (1980, pp. 120–30, 147–51) have all described progressions in how children regard the nature of parent–child relations. These are summarized in Table 7.1.

Selman reports a study in which children in the Boston area were interviewed about their beliefs about punishment. They were asked, for example, 'Why do parents sometimes punish their children? How does punishment work? What does it do for children? When parents get upset with their children they sometimes punish them.

Table 7.1 Stages in children's perceptions of parent–child relations

Selman (1980, pp. 147–51) General relationships	Damon (1977, pp. 178–9) Rationales for obedience	Harter (1982a, pp. 46–50) Harter and Barnes (1981) Parental emotions
Stage 0: Boss–servant relationship based on the child's perception of the parent as physically powerful	*Level 0-A*: Obedience is based on a primitive association between the authority's commands and the self's desires	*Stage 1*: Some event which evokes a child emotion is seen to in the parent
Stage 1: Caretaker–helper relationship based on physical reciprocity (they do things for each other). Punishment is viewed as a teaching device. Conflicts are caused by mistakes	*Level 0-B*: Obedience in a pragmatic fashion: commands are followed as a means of achieving desires, or to avoid actions contrary to desires	*Stage 2*: Child is the cause of emotion *Stage 3*: Events in parents' life do not involve the child yet provoke parental emotions
Stage 2: Guidance counsellor–need satisfier relationship based on reciprocal psychological and emotional support. Punishment is viewed as a method of communication. Conflicts are understood to be caused by genuine differences of opinion	*Level 1-A*: Obedience is based on the child's respect for authority figure's social or physical power which is invested with an authority of omnipotence and omniscience	
Stage 3: Toleration–relationship is based on a third point of view: an abstract ideal of a parent–child relationship. Children reflect on parents' personal circumstances and motivations for punishment which may not be related to the child's misbehaviour. There is an understanding that some children need to be controlled. Conflicts are seen as resolvable through third-party mediation	*Level 1-B*: Obedience is based on reciprocal exchange: one obeys because a figure has helped him in the past or because a figure otherwise 'deserves' his obedience	
	Level 2-A: Obedience is based on subject's respect for specific leadership ability and on the belief that this superior leadership ability implies concern for the welfare and rights of subordinates	
	Level 2-B: Authority is seen as a shared, consensual relation between parties adopted temporarily by one person for the welfare of all. Obedience is seen as a cooperative effort which is situation-specific rather than a general response to a specific person	

Do you get punished sometimes? Why do you think your parents punish you sometimes? Do you think your parents could bring you up without ever punishing you?'

The children's responses were coded into four 'levels'. At level 0, children are reputed not to understand the parent's motives underlying punishment, and are unable to discriminate punishment as a conscious retribution from a physical reaction to misbehaviour. At level 1, punishment is a teaching device for protecting children from danger and for setting things right. For example, children will say that punishment is justified 'Because you take out your bike, you get hit by a car, and your mother says, "Don't take out your bike"', or that children who have done something wrong 'should be paid back for it' (Selman 1980, p. 124).

At level 2, punishment is seen as a form of communication, an attempt to appeal to the child's own judgement and sense of control. Punishment is justified so that children will remember and not repeat their misbehaviour. By adolescence, most children will have reached level 3 in which, according to Selman, there is a 'mutual coordination of perspectives'. Punishment is seen to serve simultaneously the needs of parents and their children and it is recognized that parents have their lives too: 'If a kid is always screwing up, it's not just the kid who needs to see the light. The parents don't always want to be bailing him out of trouble.'

Selman proceeds to give a 'summary description of stages in conceptions of parent–child relations'. These stages form the content of the formal aspects of perspective taking referred to as 'levels'. Thus at stage 1, the child acknowledge the parent's good intentions and obedience is rationalized both to avoid punishment and out of gratitude to the parent. At stage 2 the parent–child relation is viewed as the mutual satisfaction of psychological and emotional needs coloured by the conscious knowledge that the parent's judgement is fallible. Finally, at stage 3, there is an idealized relationship between parents and children from a third person perspective which is one of tolerance and respect. The child comes to understand that close and loving relations can have an important impact on his or her own personality development, that the adult has a need to be respected as a source of authority, and that children have a need for autonomy and independence. Getting along is a matter of tolerance and respect for the other.

The Damon and the Harter stages are very similar to those levels and stages described by Selman. In particular, Harter sees the child's understanding of parental emotions as the unravelling of a childhood egocentrism: from viewing parental emotions as elicited from the same events as those that elicit child emotions to recognizing that the events which provoke parental emotions may be different.

To elicit responses at different stages, children typically have been given stories on the theme of parent–child relations. These have concerned misdemeanours committed by children, the motives underlying punishment and obedience, and the emotional reactions of parents and children to a variety of situations. On the basis of an interview, the child's responses are categorized in stages or levels. This sort of procedure may appear intuitively appealing, but it is open to a number of disconcerting questions.

Many of these arise from the technique itself which could not help but yield answers more than faintly reminiscent of Piaget's egocentrism notion. Indeed, only an extremely bold little boy or girl would say to the astonishment of an adult interviewer that 'problems which concern children and make them sad do not necessarily concern adults' or that 'adults have their own lives to lead'. The characteristics of the interview might demand that only older children or adolescents would feel comfortable with 'level/stage 3' statements. As suggested by the range of studies discussed in Chapter 4, such statements may not be within the capacity of younger children. Should they be given a recognition problem in which the task, for example, is to identify rather than enumerate the most appropriate rationale for childhood obedience, young children may prefer higher-level statements over lower ones. In this regard, a recent study by Gnepp (1983) has shown that grade 1 children can simultaneously consider conflicting emotional cues emanating from two different sources.

A related difficulty is that the interview procedure centres on an unidirectional model of social cognition. A child can give only two kinds of responses: either that the same event which affects the child causes the same emotion in the parent or that events which provoke emotions may diverge for parents and children. The extent to which the emotions of parents and children provoke divergent events is comparatively neglected. Moreover, the questions have typically dealt with the parent reacting to misbehaviour or to events which have affected the child and do not concern the great amount of time and effort which parents put into childrearing in order to prevent misbehaviour occurring in the first place. Thus the stage theory tested by the interview tends to be self-supporting. It is difficult to discover young children whose understanding of the self is a reflec-

tion of their perceptions of others according to a symbolic interactionist account because the questions do not easily allow for such
answers.

These studies do illustrate, though, the emphasis which children
of all ages give to agreement between parents and children through a
legitimized parental control. As in Chapter 5, the two-process model
of perceived control proposed by Rothbaum, Weisz, and Snyder
(1982, pp. 20–1) is relevant. First, there are primary control processes
which are characterized by attempts to understand problems toward
resolution or mastery, to predict events so as to succeed at them, to
influence chance-determined outcomes and to manipulate powerful
others. By contrast, secondary control processes involve attempts to
understand problems so as to derive from these meaning and acceptance. In the case of children, secondary control results from a
vicarious association with parental others, an identification which
reflects a desire for a 'self-defining' relationship with a powerful
person. Obedience and submissiveness is underscored by a desire to
fit in with others.

According to Rothbaum, Weisz, and Snyder (1982, p. 30), the
successful adaptiveness or adjustment of personality involves 'a
knowledge of how and when to exert the two processes of control
and how to integrate them'. As they note, this knowledge is likely to
be situationally based and it is difficult to determine the optimal
balance in all cases. For some persons and circumstances, primary
control would be more appropriate, while in others, secondary control. Some individuals value the personal achievements which are
fostered by primary control; others value the community safety
which is fostered by secondary control.

For young children, legitimized parental control would appear
most appropriately to involve secondary control processes which
later, at adolescence, become integrated with forms of primary control. In this connection, the self is a reflection of perceptions of
parents. With regard to secondary control processes, it involves a
desire to fit in and find meaning through acceptance and an identification with powerful others. This control is a foundation of primary
control processes which involve the growth of independence and
autonomy in adolescence. Bearing in mind the weaknesses of the
egocentrism concept, the implications of a lack of primary/second-
ary control can otherwise be viewed in Piagetian terms. According to
Rothbaum, Weisz, and Snyder (1982, p. 8), a rough analogy can be
drawn between this primary/secondary relationship assimilation and
accommodation as described by Piaget . . .

Assimilation denotes the tendency to perceive the environment in ways consistent with one's existing cognitive structures. In extreme cases of both assimilation and primary control, the individual, in a sense, places his or her desires above the demands of reality. In complementary fashion, accommodation is the tendency to modify one's cognitive structures in an attempt to effect a better fit with reality. As is true of secondary control in extreme accommodation the demands of reality overwhelm the self's desires.

Adjustment can be gained through some combination of secondary control and acceptance together with primary control and mastery. Either source of control can maintain the same standard of manifest moral behaviour and intellectual performance. If neither is present, maladjustment may occur. Two examples can be given as illustrations.

The first has to do with Piaget's notion of 'immanent justice', a type of secondary control illustrated by children's responses to story situations in which a child suffers a mishap after having transgressed. For example, a little boy is described as having disobeyed his mother. He later goes outside to play and while crossing a stream he walks across a bridge made out of rotten timber and falls in. In response to questions concerning the cause of the mishap, younger children often claim that the boy's disobedience caused him to suffer this consequence while older children give the naturalistic explanation that the boy fell in by chance because the bridge was weak and collapsed.

To the immanent causality and the non-immanent 'chance continguity' explanations, Karniol (1980, 1982) has added a third: a 'psychologically mediated' causal explanation in which the mishap is posited to have led to a psychological reaction that somehow produced the adversity. For example, some children might respond that the disobedient boy was so distressed by his transgression that he did not watch where he was going and check to see whether the bridge was safe.

In a recent study (Karniol 1982), it was reasoned that a belief in immanent justice should have behavioural correlates in line with Piagetian and Freudian theorizing. According to Piaget, children who believe in scientific explanations and give chance continguity responses should possess a mature mutual respect orientation and be less likely to misbehave than those who believe in immanent causality and possess a unilateral respect orientation. According to Freud (1961a)—though this may be stretching the focus of Freudian theory somewhat—the child with the strong punishing superego should also believe in psychologically mediated and immanent causality explanations. This child should not be likely to misbehave for there is a belief that everywhere forces abound which enforce obedience and administer punishment. By contrast, the child who believes in chance contiguity will steer away from such explanations. Freed from the thought that misfortune will be punished by external forces or accompanied by guilt, the chance contiguity child will now be endowed with the motive to misbehave.

The subjects were 43 Israeli children aged 10–12 years attending a school located in a mixed working-class and middle-class area. The children were given three stories designed to elicit beliefs in immanent justice: (1) stealing money from mother's purse followed by falling and hurting one's leg, (2) lying to mother and falling into a puddle and dirtying one's coat, and (3) stealing fruit from a neighbouring garden and falling off one's bike and breaking an arm. The responses were coded into the three categories of immanent causality. These were correlated with a measure of cheating on a test which was administered 1 month later.

Of the 17 children giving psychologically mediated responses, 13 cheated. Comparable numbers for immanent causality and chance contiguity were 2 out of 10 and 1 out of 7 respectively. In a follow-up study, those who offered psychologically mediated explanations often anticipated that others would experience guilt and confess after having transgressed.

One interpretation of these results follows from the writings of Adler (Beecher 1959). Guilt feelings are created by individuals because, once caught for a transgression, they are exempted from punishment. 'Our parents' stony hearts' have been softened by confessions of guilt and punishment is consequently alleviated. Beyond this interpretation which is suggested by Karniol, it can also be conjectured that the children who believe in immanent justice do not cheat as they are influenced by a type of secondary control, a desire to accept and submit to the powerful other. Personal autonomy is subordinated to parental authority. As for 'chance continguity' children, they do not cheat owing to a type of primary control. There is no need to cheat if there is a desire to attribute success to one's own effort and skill. Personal autonomy is placed above the demands of adherence to parental authority. By contrast, confession-oriented psychologically mediated responses are evidence of a lack of control, either primary or secondary.

An area in need of further study concerns the extent of conflict and agreement which the three types of children have with parents and peers. According to this analysis, those who give psychologically mediated responses should show more conflict and less agreement with others than do their immanent justice and chance continguity counterparts.

A second example of adjustment through primary and secondary control processes comes from research on adolescents. For many years, there has been a controversy regarding the issue of conflict between parents and children which is alledgedly accompanied by a crisis in the self-perceptions of the adolescent. One view is that such conflict is clearly undesirable. An alternative view shared among many clinicians and psychoanalysts (see, for example, Erikson 1968; A. Freud 1966) is that conflict to a certain extent is inevitable and normal, and some have even gone so far to claim that conflict is desirable and that a lack of conflict is abnormal.

A study by Spivack (1957) found that emotionally disturbed adolescents are significantly more likely to express a favourable attitude toward restrictive maternal childrearing practices than are non-disturbed controls, which is interpreted to suggest that 'adolescent rebellion as a positive drive for independence' is less characteristic of emotionally disturbed than of normal children. Cognitive-developmental theories (for example, Haan, Smith, and Block 1968; Kohlberg and Kramer 1969) have also looked at adolescent rebellion in a positive light. It has been suggested that such rebellion is a way-station toward attaining a mature level of moral judgement. Conventional 'law and order' morality may give way to a principled basis for moral reasoning should adolescents and young adults experience a period of cognitive conflict and rebellion against parental or societal values.

As Weiner (1970, p. 48) has observed, 'contrary to these influential views that adolescence is normally and normatively a disturbed state, considerable data suggest that the model teenager is a reasonably well-adjusted individual whose daily functioning is minimally marred by psychological incapacity'. Though such views endure (see, for example, Simmons, Rosenberg, and Rosenberg 1973), additional data from a recent longitudinal study (Dusek and Flaherty 1981) should serve somewhat to dispel the controversy.

The subjects were 330 adolescents attending schools in a suburban school district, including families of upper-class, middle-class, and lower-middle-class socioeconomic status. They were given a self-concept measure in the form of a semantic differential scale containing 21 bipolar items such as relaxed–nervous, valuable–worthless, friendly–unfriendly, and leader–follower. The adolescents were asked on three separate occasions over 3 years to read each adjective pair and to indicate their 'characteristic self' on a 1–7 scale. The anchor points were located at the extremes for each pair. Substantial continuity and stability over time was present in the subjects' ratings. There were also sex differences consistent with sex role stereotypes. Males scored higher than females on a factor of achievement and leadership and females scored higher than males on a factor of congeniality and sociability.

While the Dusek and Flaherty study did not concern the actual behaviour of adolescents as observed by parents, teachers, and peers, it is inconsistent with the notion that conflict is an inevitable or normal aspect of development. The period of *Sturm und Drang* during adolescence has no more support than the benefits for children of intrapersonal and interpersonal conflict extolled by cognitive-developmental theories. Other work as well (McCrae and Costa 1982) illustrates the stability of personality in young adulthood, middle age, and old age.

The assumption that storm and stress is a normal part of development has mistakenly led many theorists to assume that psychological disturbance in adolescence may often not warrant counselling or professional attention (Masterson 1968). Secondary control processes can provide a foundation for autonomy and independence. Any change may be smooth and gradual as Dusek and Flaherty suggest. Disturbed adolescents or delinquents may still be searching for that very secondary control, the lack of which contributes to their maladjustment and behavioural difficulties.

The development of self in childhood is partly a reflection of perceptions of parents. As a secondary control process, these involve a desire to fit in and identify with powerful others. As a foundation of primary control processes in adolescence and adulthood, these may serve to promote judgements of responsibility and a commitment to rules and principles of behaviour. According to Candee and Kohlberg (1982), judgements of responsibility which 'determine to what extent that which is morally good is also strictly necessary for the self' may provide a substantial relationship between moral reasoning and behaviour.

But though the transition to autonomy and independence does not necessarily require conflict, adolescents must come to a point at which the force of secondary control weakens in many areas of decision-making. The plea of the adolescent who wants to be adult is often: 'If I refuse to make my own decisions, I am, in merely copying my fathers, showing myself a lesser man than they; for whereas they must have initiated, I shall be merely accepting' (Hare 1952, p. 77). Some adolescents, it must be said, may go so far to accuse parents as seeking to mould completely their careers, moral judgements, and personal relationships. They may perceive oppression instead of the legitimized control associated with an idealized picture of parenthood. The struggle is to surface and become a 'creative non-victim'. In common with the aim that is frequently symbolized by the lives of characters in literature, the objective is to refuse to accept victimization and ultimately to remove its cause (Atwood 1972, pp. 38–9). The adolescent's construction of self is no longer distorted to correspond with that envisioned by powerful others. It now becomes the source of a creative, independent achievement and morality, and forms a basis for resolving personal and social problems.

8

Development as reflected by changes in the nature of parenthood: a bubble-up view

Frequently, issues in developmental psychology have been studied in isolation from context. The focus of moral development has been on children's responses to hypothetical dilemmas rather than on a 'hot' cognition of thoughts and feelings about other persons. The study of achievement has centred on reinforcement and attributions for past performance rather than others' expectations for the future. Children described as egocentric have been said to prefer permissive methods of childrearing instead of an interventionist approach which is both firm and sensitive to situations. Explanations for delinquency have been many and varied; these often have revolved around genetic and peer influences rather than effects related to the absence of control in a social context. Similarly, children's views on economic justice have been interpreted in terms of cognitive developmental stages; their perceptions of others' economic and educational achievements have been overlooked. Finally, conflict rather than agreement between intellectual strategies has been seen as a major source of development.

Ever since the two-pronged attack of the social learning and cognitive-developmental approaches on children's self-definition and identification processes, these aspects of development have received scant attention compared to that accorded to learning and 'cool' cognition. In stepping back to view the overall picture we are left with curiously impersonal accounts of development; behaviour to a considerable extent has eluded prediction. Since the issues which are of concern to the child have tended to be ignored by researchers interested in the child's responses to their own questions, results often have amounted to images in a hall of mirrors. It is probably not an overstatement to suggest that, since cool cognition fits developmental stages better than behaviour, the former has been studied at the expense of the latter. Long ago, Allport (1954) spotted this type of fallacy, deeming it the 'misplaced category' of investigation. To build a comprehensive behavioural theory requires that a picture of development be entertained from the child's point of view.

The shift away from studying constructs such as children's self-definition, identification and perceptions of others parallels changes during the past 20 years in the nature of parenthood. Commentators in the media often have suggested that the current generation of parents is not as concerned as their predecessors in expending effort at childcare and instead are more involved in developing their own selves. Bronfenbrenner (1970) has even speculated that children are now no longer brought up as much by their parents as by television.

There is a sense, however, in which the task of parenthood has become more difficult. A child places physical and emotional demands on parents. Time restrictions and financial sacrifices create strains in the husband–wife relationship. This is nothing new, but as West (1982, pp. 149–50) astutely points out, on top of the traditional pressures of parenthood, today's children are expected to possess more material goods. Financially insecure parents cannot meet these expectations easily. From an earlier age, children are exposed to values and interests which potentially conflict with the parents' own. At the same time, family size has decreased which means that fewer people have had preparation for parenthood in taking care of younger siblings.

Many adults regard childhood in any event as a time best left forgotten. Nevertheless, the consequences of this selective amnesia can be despairing and disorienting. The person who could not wait to become an adult may come to reflect:

How quickly I galloped out of my distant childhood, until I reached the white palace of old age, and found it wide and empty. I can no longer see my road's beginning. . . . The caravan of days, from afar will move on its way, from nothingness to nothingness without me.

Vogel (1981, p. 527)

Changes in the nature of childhood are linked inextricably with changes in the nature of parenthood. The growth in the numbers of working mothers has changed the role of the father. The rising incidence of separation and divorce has created an increasing number of one-parent families some of which are headed by fathers. These two non-traditional facets of contemporary family life require a bubble-up perspective on socioeconomic conditions and the quality of parent–child relations.

Non-traditional family arrangements

Maternal employment

The effects of maternal employment can be considered with respect to children's perceptions of the mother and father. Elder (1974, p. 95), in commenting upon the low community status of deprived families, states that:

The implications of status loss for relations between father and child are well-documented in the research literature, especially for sons. The attractiveness of father, as a model and source of values, is related to his occupational status: the higher the status, the stronger the attraction. Though mother's social prestige is derived in part from family status, the association is generally not as strong in children's perceptions. These relationships suggest two main outcomes of economic deprivation in both social classes: compared to fathers in nondeprived families, the deprived father is regarded less favorably by children and is ranked lower than mother by boys and girls.

Elder's obvervations pertain to deprived families during the Depression of the 1930s, and are consistent as well with the effects of economic deprivation on father–child relations of low-income families in the postwar era. In this regard, probably the most notable recent changes in the nature of the workforce has been the increased number of working mothers (L. W. Hoffman 1979). The rapid growth in maternal employment after 1940 is statistically as dramatic as the rapid proliferation in unemployment during the 1930s. In 1940, about 10 per cent or 1.5 million of American women with preschool and school-aged children were employed. By 1970, the figure had increased to 42 per cent of all mothers, and by 1974 nearly 14 million or 47 per cent of mothers were employed (US Department of Commerce, 1979). At present, the working mother is in the clear majority and the numbers are still growing.

Maternal employment is associated with variations in power between the parents, and is related to children's perceptions of the father. In the middle-class family, mothers often work out of a desire to pursue a challenging career and not for financial reasons alone. By contrast, the mother in the low-income family often works at unchallenging or menial jobs and financial reasons can be more important. Maternal employment may be perceived to imply that the father has failed in his duty to provide for his family (L. W. Hoffman 1974, p. 208).

Despite research over the past 20 years which has indicated that maternal employment in low-income families is accompanied by strains in the relationship between sons and fathers, a comprehensive understanding of these influences is still lacking. Maternal employment effects, however, can be seen as similar to those of depression unemployment in increasing the mother's stature relative to that of the father.

In an early study at the University of Michigan, Douvan (1963) found that adolescent boys from working-class families chose their fathers as ideals less frequently than do other boys, though it must be cautioned that working-class boys may respond less favourably toward both parents. Similarly, McCord, McCord, and Thurber (1963) examined the records of 149 boys who participated in a community programme for disadvantaged youngsters living in the Boston area. Counsellors visited the boys at home, school, and play for an average of 5 years when they were between the ages of 10 and 15. The boys were divided into two groups according to whether or not their mothers were employed, and the groups were subdivided further according to family stability. A family was considered unstable by virtue of the father's 'criminal, alcoholic, promiscuous, or blatantly irresponsible behavior'. A measure of attitudes toward the father was derived both from statements about, and behaviour toward, the father. While boys whose mothers worked showed a slight tendency to disapprove more of the father, disapproval was most strongly related to instability. Of the 60 boys from stable homes, only nine indicated disapproval of their fathers; the comparable number of the 89 boys from unstable homes was 32.

The effects of maternal employment on adolescents' perceptions of the father were investigated further by Propper (1972) using a sample of 68 boys from working-class homes in Toronto. Fathers with employed wives tended to be evaluated more negatively than fathers with unemployed wives. In response to the question, 'What man do you admire most?', 15 out of the group of 40 boys whose mothers did not work expressed admiration for their fathers in contrast to five out of the group of 28 whose mothers were employed. The difference between the two groups was not significant, and the groups expressed a similar admiration for the mother.

Two more recent Canadian studies using 10-year-olds and adolescents as subjects also indicate no significant differences in children's evaluations of the father relating to maternal employment (Gold and Andres 1978*a* and *b*). The strain in the father–son relationship in a working-class family where the mother is employed was evident only in fathers' claims that they have problems with their 10-year-old sons' behaviour at school, and in fathers' ratings of their son as uncooperative and unambitious (Gold and Andres 1978*b*, p. 78). Though maternal employment in the modern working-class family does not change children's perceptions of the father in absolute terms of adulation, it may elevate the mother above the father in relative terms which in turn gives rise to the father's resentment towards his family. Indeed, working-class husbands are significantly less likely to approve of their wife's employment than are middle-class husbands.

None of the studies using adolescents as subjects have made direct comparisons of children's perceptions of mothers and fathers, though maternal employment can be assumed to have shifted the power of the mother in the marriage and in her relationship with her children. Interview studies with married couples have long suggested that working wives make more of the important decisions in the family than their non-working counterparts, particularly in working-class homes (Heer 1958).

In some families, either the mother or father is perceived by the child as dominant; in others, conjugal relationships are seen as egalitarian. To examine whether the perceived distribution of power between the parents is related to children's 'identifications', Bowerman and Bahr (1973) gave questionnaires to over 18 000 high-school students in Ohio and North Carolina. Their identifications were measured by responses to questions such as 'Would you like to be the kind of person your mother (father) is?' and 'How much do you depend on your mother's (father's) opinions to influence your ideas of right and wrong?' As a measure of power, the students were asked 'When important family problems come up, which parent usually has the most influence in making the decision?'

Regardless of perceived power, girls had higher identification scores with mothers than with fathers. The difference was greatest when the father was perceived as weaker and least when he was perceived as dominant. By contrast, boys identified more strongly with whichever parent is perceived to be dominant. Thus a proposition which remains a hypothesis only is that maternal employment affects children's parental identification by altering the balance of power in the family.

The father's effectiveness as an involved parent

Increasing maternal employment has been accompanied by a greater participation of the father in childrearing. A growing body of research suggests that the father's involvement in what traditionally has been assumed to be the primary prerogative of the mother can foster his children's social and cognitive development. In short, fathers in circumstances of economic change are often faced with taking on increased childrearing duties owing to the mother's career aims and possibly their own unemployment. Many have proved themselves to be capable as children's primary caretakers and have demonstrated the potential of the father to adapt well to the conflict in filling the mother's traditional role.

The undesirable effects of economic change on the father may be mitigated by the extent and nature of the father's involvement with his children and his social class background. In Gold and Andres' (1978a) study of the effects of maternal employment on 10-year-olds, estimates of the quality of the father's involvement with his children were given by both the father and the mother. These measures were correlated significantly with children's self-reports of personal worth, social skills, self-reliance, and school relations. In line with children's favourable appraisals of adult intervention discussed in Chapter 4 of this volume, positive child characteristics were associated with the fathers' self-reported involvement in disciplinary matters.

Radin's (1972, 1973) studies have shown a significant relationship between fathers' participation in childrearing and their sons' cognitive development. Father–son interaction during interviews was tape-recorded and scored for fathers' nurturance toward their sons. In general, nurturance was correlated significantly with boys' intelligence test scores. Though the correlations between the nurturance measures and IQ diminished in retests 1 year later, some remained statistically significant. The quality of paternal involvement in childrearing is possibly an antecedent of boys' intellectual functioning.

The nature of the father's care resembles that of the mother. Despite the belief in a maternal instinct which is frequently held by both parents, children can be securely attached to either the mother or father (or both) and fathers can do many household tasks, including feeding of the children, as well as mothers (Parke 1979, 1981). While in the traditional Western family much of the father's influence on the child is indirect in that the relationship between the parents affects the nature of the mother's relationship with the child

(M. L. Hoffman 1963), the father as the child's primary caretaker is quite similar to the mother, particularly in interactions involving smiling and imitation (Field 1978). There would seem to be no reason why fathers should not perform equally affectionate and warm roles and be every bit as 'motherly' as actual mothers.

The research on fathers in the two-parent family points to the potential effectiveness of the father as single parent. But though the effects of divorce on children's cognitive and social development have been intensively researched (Kurdek 1981), only a small amount of attention has been directed to the effects of specific custodial arrangements and access. Research on the effects of joint custody is also lacking (Clingempeel and Reppucci 1982).

In their pioneering study, Santrock and Warshak (1979) compared children aged 6–11 years from father-custody homes, mother-custody homes, and from intact homes. Both parents and children were given a variety of measures, including rating scales and projective tasks. The custodial parent and child also participated in structured videotaped sessions in which they were asked to plan an activity and discuss major problems of the family. Children living with the same-sex parent (that is, father-custody boys and mother-custody girls) appeared better adjusted on those measures than the children living with the opposite sex parent, and boys in father-custody families were better adjusted than those from two-parent families. As the investigators state, however, these results are tentative and preliminary. For example, the groups were not equated for family income. Stress arising from financial problems in the mother-custody homes without the income of a father could have influenced the results.

The degree of marital conflict in a large number of two-parent families may exceed that between separated or divorced marriage partners (Santrock *et al.* 1982). Clearly, conflict is associated with a lack of behavioural control in boys (Block, Block, and Morrison 1981). Thus it is vital that a distinction be made between high and low marital conflict in two-parent families before making a comparison of two-parent and single-parent custodial arrangements. Previous studies have mostly neglected this issue. Moreover, the degree to which the parents participating in such studies are representative of separated and divorced parents in general is usually unknown. For these reasons, more intensive and carefully controlled research is needed.

Though the father can be as effective as the mother in either the two-parent or single-parent family, the actual extent to which fathers are disposed toward becoming involved as primary care-takers again appears to be related to social class and to the family's situation. The relationships between sons' intellectual functioning and paternal nurturance found in Radin's (1972, 1973) studies held only for middle-class fathers and their sons. No relationships were found for working-class fathers who displayed significantly less interaction and nurturance toward sons on measures of paternal involvement than did their middle-class counterparts.

Participation in many childrearing activities may be incompatible with the masculine image to which many working-class men ascribe. G. Russell (1978) used the Bem Sex-Role Inventory to assess the sex-role preferences of fathers in relation in their involvement in day-to-day childrearing activities such as feeding, bathing, and changing nappies. Information from a joint interview with the mother and father indicated that fathers classified as masculine were significantly less likely to be involved in day-to-day care than those who were not sex-typed. Since androgyny may be harder to achieve for the working-class father, possibly he is less disposed toward an involvement in childrearing than his middle-class counterpart. As noted in Chapter 6 of this volume, however, androgyny might not necessarily be a desirable state for a parent.

Family support and the responsibilities of children and adolescents: a bubble-up proposal

Changing socioeconomic circumstances have focused attention on the bubble-up effects of combating economic deprivation through support for fathers and mothers in the family context. In a longitu-dinal study by Gore (1978), married blue-collar workers who became unemployed owing to a plant shutdown were asked to report at five points in time on the degree of perceived economic depriva-tion and supportive relations with their wives, friends, and relations. Those perceived as supported by others while unemployed reported significantly less psychological and physical health problems than did those who perceived themselves to be unsupported. Even when the unsupported found jobs again, their perceptions of economic deprivation remained greater than the supported.

The Gore study is illustrative of how the family can ameliorate the plight of the economically deprived. In particular, since the un-employed may not have the concern and sympathy of children and adolescents' efforts could be directed toward broadening youth's understanding of those in economic need. In the case of economically deprived families, this form of intervention might affect the quality of parent–child relations through cushioning the impact of abusive parenting on later social-cognitive development (Barahal, Waterman, and Martin 1981; Straker and Jacobson 1981).

A bubble-up approach which directs income to deprived families is not necessarily incompatible with a trickle-down one. Effects which permeate downwards to widen the level of economic deprivation could rebound upwards in bubbling up to depress further the level of business income, investment, and unemployment. Indeed the spiral-type nature of a deepening economic recession would seem to bear out this contention. A degree of mutual causation might occur with deprivation and business income determining each other.

Some economists on the one hand argue that a bubble-up approach to social welfare is inflationary. By maintaining what is regarded by some as a high level of taxation, it strifles the incentive to work and therefore lowers both productivity and investment, creating greater economic deprivation in the longer term. Dworkin (1983, pp. 34–5) on the other hand forcefully rejects this argument as a careless, absurd, and unjust rationale to ignore the poor now:

People laid off for several years, with no effective retraining, are very unlikely to recoup their losses later, particularly if their psychological losses are counted. Children denied adequate nutrition or any effective chance at higher education will suffer permanent loss even if the economy follows the most optimistic path of recovery. Some of those who are denied jobs and welfare now, particularly the elderly, will in any case not live long enough to share in that recovery, however general it turns out to be. . . . The children of the poor must not be stinted of education or otherwise locked into positions at the bottom of society. Otherwise their parents' loyalty to them acts not as a bridge but as a bar to any identification with the future these parents are meant to cherish.

All the same, bubble-up strategies inspired by Keynesian econmomic theory may be no better at ameliorating economic deprivation than are trickle-down policies. As Cook and Pearlman (1981, p. 377) remark, the effectiveness of bubble-up in Western countries has been so difficult to determine because it rarely has been practised alone without trickle-down policies as well. Nor has a concerted effort been made to ensure that bubble-up resources are received by specific types of needy persons who might have been among the greatest beneficiaries. There may be groups of 'backwash poor' who remain continually untouched by programmes designed to eradicate poverty.

With regard to the validity of a bubble-up model, economic deprivation, either as a drop in income relative to previous affluence or as income below a community average, may be an antecedent of marital conflict and divorce (Becker, Landes, and Michael 1977; Brandwein, Brown, and Fox 1974; L. W. Hoffman 1977; Ross and Sawhill 1975, p. 56). In an important study, Greenberg and Wolf (1982) found that marital disruption is an antecedent of children's subsequent poor economic performance as adults. This effect is mainly attributed to the mother's increased economic deprivation. According to Greenberg and Wolf, the adolescent sons of mothers who receive an adequate compensation for the earnings of absent fathers are likely not to show a decline in their earnings later as adults. Should the mother's compensation be insufficient, sons' earnings are likely to fall.

The Greenberg and Wolf study is a first attempt to examine the economic consequences to children of conflict between the mother and the father. If their analysis is correct, the economic and social stability of the family could in itself be viewed as an objective of a bubble-up welfare policy. Stability would be envisioned to increase the purchasing power of the poor and their offspring, increasing business income, investment and employment opportunities with more relative and absolute equality for all. Indeed, the benefits of negative income tax programmes aimed to assist single parents cannot be ruled out (Groenewald, Tuma, and Hannan 1980, p. 672).

A range of bubble-up programmes could be integrated with trickle-down incentives to industry. To take one example, the work experiences of children and adolescents could be stimulated toward enhancing perceptions of parents and reducing conflict in the family.

To give youth the opportunity to participate in responsible activities may contribute to the development of a concern for others (Staub 1979). Adolescents who engage in responsible economic activities through part-time work experiences can develop more sensitivity to the stress involved in their parents' jobs if employed, together with a deeper respect for their parents' economic difficulties (Steinberg *et al.* 1981).

The effects of part-time work on adolescent development have recently been investigated in a series of studies by Steinberg, Greenberger, and their co-workers (Greenberger and Steinberg 1983;

Greenberger *et al.* 1980; Steinberg *et al.* 1982). The sample surveyed over a 1-year period consisted of tenth and eleventh-graders attending high school in Orange County, California. In response to questions about how close they felt to their families, working boys generally reported increased closeness in contrast to working girls who reported decreased closeness. The sharing of adult work experiences may serve to mellow boys' perceptions of their parents; by comparison, girls who decide to work may already be predisposed to their feeling less close to the family. Working, if viewed as an act of independence, may increase the girl's sense of autonomy. An area in need of further study is the relationship of maternal employment to working adolescents' perceptions of their parents. Work responsibility can contribute to family support and may bubble-up in the form of increased economic performance.

One other ramification of adolescent employment is suggested by Shore and Massimo (1979). In a 15-year vocationally oriented programme, delinquent boys were given assistance in job placement together with job training and psychotherapy. As adults, these former delinquents demonstrated more stable social relationships and work histories than controls, although the numbers of boys in the programme were small.

Some contemporary issues

Both children's understanding of economic arrangements and the part-time employment of adolescents constitute a rich agenda for research (Steinberg and Greenberger 1980). As Gurney and Taylor (1981) point out, economic deprivation in general presents research issues which are both myriad and daunting. A void remains in knowledge about the quality of parent–child relations under particular circumstances of deprivation when, for example, father and adolescent son are both unemployed or when one has found employment and the other remains involuntarily without work. Little is known, for example, about the effects on parent–child relations of parental underemployment when workers are employed in occupations which underutilize their skills. Moreover, little is known about how younger children can be given responsible activities which serve to foster understanding and moderate the economic strain experienced by adults.

While studies of the Great Depression have entered into some of these issues (Eisenberg and Lazarsfeld 1938; Elder 1974), the effects of economic deprivation in the different industrial conditions of the 1970s and 1980s have generally not been the object of a detailed examination (Fraser 1981; M. Jahoda 1979). The nature of technological change and the increased rate of welfare state benefits are two of the many characteristics which differentiate the 1980s from the 1930s. The effects of unemployment on parent–child relations owing to industry-specific technological changes in the 1980s may differ from effects associated with a general economic depression.

To this end, a shift in focus is required both on the part of those to be studied and on the part of investigators. In the former case, employers in Western countries have generally tended to assume that the work and family worlds of their employees do not conflict. Since work has been viewed as masculine and family responsibility as feminine, work and family issues have been studied separately with little regard given to the other. Economic policies, for example, have been studied with regard to their effects on inflation and unemployment with scant attention to children's self-definition, identification, and perceptions of their parents. There is even resistance to studying how stress at work affects the family and vice versa— though the pressure of long working hours, extensive travel and transfer relocations certainly endangers family stability (Renshaw 1976). Studies of the economic system and its relation to the family would be facilitated with a softening of this resistance, and would contribute to the development of government and organizational policies designed to enhance parents' participation in the workforce by making provision for family responsibilities, for example, through the implementation of daycare programmes. Eekelaar (1984) reviews European social policies designed to foster the family and economic roles of parents. The interdependence of roles in Japan, with its merits and shortcomings, provides a context for further investigation.

Future research would be aided as well by the adoption of a broader approach to psychological issues. To connect psychological processes with social and historical events would serve to recapture the richness of parent–child relations in many of its most important contexts. The relationships between work and the family would be enlightened through an approach which views parent–child relations as developing within the context of an interdependent community rather than within a self-contained unit (Belsky 1981).

A theoretical model which draws from Cook and Pearlman (1981) is illustrated in Fig. 8.1. Trickle-down effects permeate downwards to affect worker satisfaction. Workers, of course, are also often parents and parental self-concept is based on occupational success and achievement. It relates to the use of disciplinary techniques. Children's perceptions of parents and parenthood and their definition of self in relation to others are influenced by parents' sensitivity to situations. These child attributes mediate behaviour. Perceptions and parental expectations and discipline techniques are mutual influences on each other.

Economic activity translates into bubble-up effects with child attributes and behaviour contributing directly to parents' self-concept and indirectly to their motivation as workers and consumers. Increasing revenue in the private and public sectors leads to new investment and new jobs and, to complete the cycle, ultimately

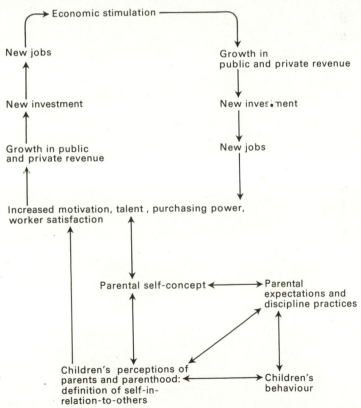

Fig. 8.1 Parent–child relations in a socioeconomic context.

trickles down in assisting to provide a strong basis for family relationships. Similar effects occur once children enter the workplace
as adolescents, and may be enhanced through family-support programmes.

In order to investigate the workings of this type of model, more
longitudinal studies are needed. Trickle-down and bubble-up policies can be evaluated not only as they affect adults in work settings
but the child within the family microsystem. This will not be a simple task, and we must be wary of the fool's gold of quick success. Yet
though such research involves pitfalls in the pursuit of a daunting
breadth of scholarship and awaits more satisfactory techniques for
analyzing longitudinal data, the issues are certainly worthy of study.

Through these means, a more comprehensive knowledge of the
relationship between economic deprivation and the quality of
parent–child relations would be gained. A basis could be provided
for formulating an interventionist and transformative developmental psychology, aimed toward promoting both economic achievement and social welfare.

References

Aberle, D. F. and Naegele, K. D. (1952). Middle-class fathers' occupational role and attitudes toward children. *American Journal of Orthopsychiatry*, **22**, 366–78.

Acock, A. C. and Bengston, V. L. (1980). Socialization and attribution processes: actual versus perceived similarity among parents and youth. *Journal of Marriage and the Family*, **42**, 501–15.

Adams, J. (1965). Inequity in social exchange. In *Advances in experimental social psychology*, Vol. 2 (ed. L. Berkowitz). Academic Press, New York.

Adelson, J., Green, B., and O'Neil, R. P. (1969). Growth of the idea of law in adolescence. *Developmental Psychology*, **1**, 327–32.

Allport, G. W. (1954). *The nature of prejudice*. Addison-Wesley, Reading, Mass.

Appel, Y. H. (1977). Developmental differences in children's perception of maternal socialization behavior. *Child Development*, **48**, 1689–93.

Armentrout, J. A. and Burger, G. K. (1972). Children's reports of parental childrearing behavior at five grade levels. *Developmental Psychology*, **7**, 44–8.

Atwood, M. (1972). *Survival*. Anansi, Toronto.

Babad, E. Y., Inbar, J., and Rosenthal, R. (1982). Teachers' judgment of students' potential as a function of teachers' susceptibility to biasing information. *Journal of Personality and Social Psychology*, **42**, 541–7.

Baldus, B. and Tribe, V. (1978). The development of perceptions and evaluations of social inequality among public school children. *Canadian Review of Sociology and Anthropology*, **15**, 50–60.

Baldwin, J. M. (1896). *Social and ethical interpretations in mental development*. Macmillan, New York. 2nd edition (1973) Arno Press, New York.

—— (1906). *Mental development in the child and the race*, 3rd edition. Macmillan, London.

Bandura, A. (1969). Social-learning theory of identificatory processes. In *Handbook of socialization theory and research* (ed. D. A. Goslin). Rand McNally, Chicago.

—— (1978). The self-system in reciprocal determinism. *American Psychologist*, **33**, 344–58.

—— (1982). The self and mechanisms of agency. In *Psychological perspectives on the self*, Vol. 1 (ed. J. Suls). L. Erlbaum, Hillsdale, NJ.

Bandura, A. (1983). Temporal dynamics and decomposition of reciprocal determinism: a reply to Philips and Orton. *Psychological Review*, **90**, 166–70.

Banks, M. H. and Jackson, P. R. (1982). Unemployment and risk of minor psychiatric disorder in young people: cross-sectional and longitudinal evidence. *Psychological Medicine*, **12**, 789–98.

Barahal, R. M., Waterman, J., and Martin, H. P. (1981). The social cognitive development of abused children. *Journal of Consulting and Clinical Psychology*, **49**, 508–16.

Bauer, P. T. (1981). *Equality, the third world, and economic delusion*. Weidenfeld and Nicolson, London.

Baumrind, D. (1973). The development of instrumental competence through socialization. In *Minnesota symposia on child psychology*, Vol. 7. (ed. A. D. Pick). University of Minnesota Press, Minneapolis.

—— (1982). Are androgynous individuals more effective persons and parents? *Child Development*, **53**, 44–75.

—— (1983*a*). Rejoinder to Lewis's reinterpretation of parental firm control effects: are authoritative parents really harmonious? *Psychological Bulletin*, **94**, 132–42.

—— (1983*b*). Specious causal attributions in the social sciences: the reformulated stepping-stone theory of heroin use as an exemplar. *Journal of Personality and Social Psychology*, **45**, 1289–98.

Becker, G. S., Landes, E. M., and Michael, R. T. (1977). An economic analysis of marital instability. *Journal of Political Economy*, **85**, 1141–87.

Beecher, W. (1959) Guilt feelings: masters of our fates on our servants? In *Essays in individual psychology* (eds. K. G. Adler and D. Deutsch). Grove Press, New York.

Bell, R. Q. (1968). A reinterpretation of the direction of effect in studies of socialization. *Psychological Review*, **75**, 81–95.

—— and Harper, L. (1977). *Child effects on adults*. L. Erlbaum, Hillsdale, NJ.

Belle, D. (1980). Mothers and their children: a study of low-income families. In *The evolving female: women in psychosocial context* (ed. C. L. Heckerman). Human Sciences Press, New York.

Belsky, J. (1981). Early human experience: a family perspective. *Developmental Psychology*, **17**, 3–23.

—— Steinberg, L. D., and Walker, A. (1982). The ecology of daycare. In *Nontraditional families: parenting and child development* (ed. M. E. Lamb), L. Erlbaum, Hillsdale, NJ.

Bem, D. (1972). Self-perception theory. In *Advances in experimental social psychology*, Vol 6 (ed L. Berkowitz). Academic Press, New York.

Bem, S. L. (1974). The measurement of psychological androgyny. *Journal of Consulting and Clinical Psychology*, **42**, 155–62.

Berg-Cross, L. G. (1975). Intentionality, degree of damage, and moral judgments. *Child Development*, **46**, 970–4.

Bettleheim, B. (1943). Individual and mass behavior in extreme situations. *Journal of Abnormal and Social Psychology*, **38**, 417–52.

Bixenstine, V. E., DeCorte, M. S., and Bixenstine, B. A. (1976). Conformity to peer-sponsored misconduct at four grade levels. *Developmental Psychology*, **12**, 226–36.

Blasi, A. (1980). Bridging moral cognition and moral action: a critical review of the literature. *Psychological Bulletin*, **88**, 1–45.

Blatt, M. M. and Kohlberg, L. (1975). The effects of classroom moral discussion upon children's level of moral judgment. *Journal of Moral Education*, **2**, 129–61.

Block, J. H. (1983). Differential premises arising from differential socialization of the sexes. *Child Development*, **54**, 1335–54.

—— Block, J., and Morrison, A. (1981). Parental agreement–disagreement on child-rearing orientations and gender-related personality correlates in children. *Child Development*, **52**, 965–74.

Bolstad, O. D. and Johnson, S. M. (1977). The relationship between teachers' assessment of students and the students' actual behavior in the classroom. *Child Development*, **48**, 570–8.

Boucher, J. and Osgood, C. E. (1969). The Pollyana hypothesis. *Journal of Verbal Learning and Verbal Behavior*, **8**, 1–8.

Bowerman, C. E. and Bahr, S. J. (1973). Conjugal power and adolescent identification with parents. *Sociometry*, **36**, 366–77.

Bradley, R. H., Caldwell, B. M., and Elardo, R. (1979). Home environment and cognitive development in the first 2 years: a cross-lagged panel analysis. *Developmental Psychology*, **15**, 246–50.

Brandwein, R. A., Brown, C. A., and Fox, E. M. (1974). Women and children last: the social situation of divorced women and their families. *Journal of Marriage and the Family*, **36**, 498–514.

Bretherton, I. and Beeghly, M. (1982). Talking about internal states: the acquisition of an explicit theory of mind. *Developmental Psychology*, **18**, 906–21.

Brislin, R. W. (1980). Translation and content-analysis of oral and written material. In *Handbook of cross cultural psychology*, Vol. 2, Methodology (ed. H. C. Triandis and J. W. Berry). Allyn and Bacon, Boston.

Bronfenbrenner, U. (1960). Freudian theories of identification and their derivatives. *Child Development*, **31**, 15–40.

—— (1970). *The worlds of childhood*. Russell Sage Foundation, New York.

—— (1977). Toward an experimental ecology of human development. *American Psychologist*, **32**, 514–32.

—— (1979). *The ecology of human development*. Harvard University Press, Cambridge, Mass.

Broughton, J. M. (1981). The genetic psychology of James Mark Baldwin. *American Psychologist*, **36**, 396–407.

Brown, G. W., Bhrolchain, M. N., and Harris, T. (1975). Social class and psychiatric disturbance among women in an urban population. *Sociology*, **9**, 225–54.

Brown, L. B. and Lallijee, M. (1981). Young persons' conceptions of criminal events. *Journal of Moral Education*, **10**, 105–12.

Brown, M. and Madge, N. (1982). *Despite the welfare state*. Heinemann, London.

Bryant, P. E. (1982). The role of conflict and of agreement between intellectual strategies in children's ideas about measurement. *British Journal of Psychology*, **73**, 243–51.

Burger, G. K. and Armentrout, J. A. (1971). A factor analysis of fifth and sixth graders' reports of parental childrearing behavior. *Developmental Psychology*, **4**, 483.

Bussey, K. and Maughan, B. (1982). Gender differences in moral reasoning. *Journal of Personality and Social Psychology*, **42**, 701–6.

Campbell, A., Converse, P. E., and Rodgers, W. L. (1976). *The quality of American life: perceptions, evaluations, and satisfactions*. Russell Sage Foundation, New York.

Candee, D. and Kohlberg, L. (1982). *The relationship of moral judgment to moral action*. Paper presented at the Annual Meetings of the American Psychological Association, Washington, DC.

Carey, P. (1981). *Bliss*. University of Queensland Press, Brisbane.

Caudill, W. A. (1973). The influence of social structure and culture on human behaviour in modern Japan. *Journal of Nervous and Mental Disease*, **157**, 240–57.

Chandler, T. A., Wolf, F. M., Cook, B., and Dugovics, D. A., (1980). Parental correlates of locus of control in fifth graders: an attempt at experimentation in the home. *Merrill-Palmer Quarterly*, **26**, 183–95.

Chodorow, N. (1978). *The reproduction of mothering*. University of California Press, Berkeley.

Clarke, R. V. G. (ed.) (1978). *Tackling vandalism*. Home Office Research Study 47. HMSO, London.

Clingempeel, W. G. and Reppucci, N. D. (1982). Joint custody after divorce: major issues and goals for research. *Psychological Bulletin*, **91**, 102–27.

Cohn, A. and Udolf, R. (1979). *The criminal justice system and its psychology*. Van Nostrand Reinhold, New York.

Coie, J. D., Dodge, K. A., and Coppotelli, H. (1982). Dimensions and types of social status: a cross-age perspective. *Developmental Psychology*, **18**, 557–70.

Colby, A., Kohlberg, L., Gibbs, J., and Lieberman, M. (1983). A longitudinal study of moral judgment. *Monographs of the Society for Research in Child Development*, **48** (1–2), Serial no. 200.

Cole, R. E. (1979). *Work, mobility, and participation: A comparative study of American and Japanese industry*. University of California Press, Berkeley.

Connell, R. W. (1970). Class consciousness in childhood. *Australian and New Zealand Journal of Sociology*, **6**, 87–99.

Connell, R. W. (1977). *Ruling class, ruling culture*. Cambridge University Press, Cambridge.

Conroy, M., Hess, R. D., Azuma, H., and Kashiwagi, K. (1980). Maternal strategies for regulating children's behavior: Japanese and American families. *Journal of Cross-Cultural Psychology*, **11**, 153–72.

Cook, T. D. and Pearlman, B. (1981). The relationship of economic growth to inequality in the distribution of income. In *The justice motive in social behavior* (eds. M. J. Lerner and S. C. Lerner). Plenum, New York.

Cooper, H. M., Burger, J. M., and Good, T. L. (1981). Gender differences in the academic locus of control beliefs of young children. *Journal of Personality and Social Psychology*, **40**, 562–72.

Cortese, A. J. (1984). Standard issue scoring of moral reasoning: a critique. *Merrill-Palmer Quarterly*, **30**, 227–46.

Covington, M. V. and Omelich, C. L. (1979). Are causal attributions causal? A path analysis of the cognitive model of achievement motivation. *Journal of Personality and Social Psychology*, **37**, 1487–1504.

—— (1984). An empirical examination of Weiner's critique of attribution theory. *Journal of Educational Psychology*, **76**, 1214–25.

Crandall, V. C., Katkovsky, W., and Crandall, V. J. (1965). Children's beliefs in their own control of reinforcements in intellectual-academic achievement situations. *Child Development*, **36**, 91–109.

Dalenberg, C. J., Bierman, K. L., and Furman, W. (1984). A re-examination of developmental changes in causal attributions. *Developmental Psychology*, **20**, 575–83.

Damon, W. (1975). Early conceptions of positive justice as related to the development of logical operations. *Child Development*, **46**, 301–12.

—— (1977). *The social world of the child*. Jossey-Bass, San Francisco.

—— and Killen, M. (1982). Peer interaction and the process of change in children's moral reasoning. *Merrill-Palmer Quarterly*, **28**, 347–67.

Danziger, K. (1971). *Socialization*. Penguin, Harmondsworth.

Darley, J. M., Klosson, E. C., and Zanna, M. P. (1978). Intentions and their contexts in the moral judgments of children. *Child Development*, **49**, 66–74.

Davidson, P., Turiel, E., and Black, A. (1983). The effects of stimulus familiarity on the use of criteria and justifications in children's social reasoning. *British Journal of Developmental Psychology*, **1**, 49–65.

Davies, M. and Kandel, D. B. (1981). Parental and peer influences on adolescents' educational plans: some further evidence. *American Journal of Sociology*, **87**, 363–87.

Deaux, K. (1984). From individual differences to social categories: analysis of a decade's research on gender. *American Psychologist*, **39**, 105–16.

Derber, C. (1978). Unemployment and the entitled worker: job-entitlement and radical political attitudes among the youthful unemployed. *Social Problems*, **26**, 26–37.

DeVos, G. (1973). *Socialization for achievement*. University of California Press, Berkeley.

Dienstbier, R. A., Hillman, D., Lehnhoff, J., Hillman, J., and Valkenaar, M. C. (1975). An emotion-attribution approach to moral behavior: Interfacing cognitive and avoidance theories of moral development. *Psychological Review*, **82**, 299–315.

Dix, T. and Grusec, J. E. (1983). Parent influence techniques: an attributional analysis. *Child Development*, **54**, 645–52.

Dooley, D. and Catalano, R. (1980). Economic change as a cause of behavioral disorder. *Psychological Bulletin*, **87**, 450–68.

Douvan, E. (1963). Employment and the adolescent. In *The employed mother in America* (ed. F. I. Nye and L. W. Hoffman). Rand McNally, Chicago.

—— and Adelson, J. (1966). *The adolescent experience*. Wiley, New York.

Dusek, J. B. and Flaherty, J. F. (1981). The development of the self-concept during the adolescent years. *Monographs of the Society for Research in Child Development*, **46**, Serial no. 191.

Dweck, C. S., Davidson, W., Nelson, S., and Enna, B. (1978). Sex differences in learned helplessness. II. The contingencies of evaluative feedback in the classroom. III. An experimental analysis. *Developmental Psychology*, **14**, 268–76.

Dworkin, R. (1983). Why liberals should believe in equality. *New York Review of Books*, **30** (1), 32–4.

Eccles (Parsons), J. (1983). Expectancies, values, and academic behaviors. In *Achievement and achievement motives* (ed. J. T. Spence). Freeman, San Francisco.

—— Adler, T., and Meece, J. L. (1984). Sex differences in achievement: a test of alternate theories. *Journal of Personality and Social Psychology*, **46**, 26–43.

Eekelaar, J. (1984). *Family law and social policy*, 2nd edition. Weidenfeld and Nicolson, London.

Eisenberg, N. and Lennon, R. (1983). Sex differences in empathy and related capacities. *Psychological Bulletin*, **94**, 100–31.

Eisenberg, P. and Lazarsfeld, P. F. (1938). The psychological effects of unemployment. *Psychological Bulletin*, **35**, 358–90.

Elder, G. H., Jr. (1974). *Children of the Great Depression*. University of Chicago Press, Chicago.

—— (1979). Historical change in life patterns and personality. *Life-span Development and Behavior*, **2**, 117–59.

—— and Rockwell, R. C. (1979). Economic depression and postwar opportunity in men's lives: A study of life patterns and mental health. In *Research in community and mental health*, Vol. 1 (ed. R. G. Simmons). JAI Press, Greenwich, Conn.

Elkind, D. and Weiner, I. B. (1978). *Development of the child*. Wiley, New York.

Elkins, J. and Andrews, R. J. (1974). *St. Lucia Reading Comprehension Test*. Teaching and Testing Resources, Brisbane, Australia.

Emprey, L. T. (1978). *American delinquency: its meaning and construction.* Dorsey, Homeword, Ill.

Endler, N. S. (1966). Estimating variance components from mean squares for random and mixed effects analysis of variance models. *Perceptual and Motor Skills*, **22**, 559–70.

—— and Hunt, J. McV. (1968). S-R inventories of hostility and comparisons of the proportions of variance from persons, responses, and situations for hostility and anxiousness. *Journal of Personality and Social Psychology*, **9**, 309–15.

Enright, R. D., Enright, W. F., and Lapsley, D. K. (1981). Distributive justice and social class: a replication. *Developmental Psychology*, **17**, 826–32.

Epstein, S. (1980). The stability of behavior: II. Implications for psychological research. *American Psychologist*, **35**, 790–806.

Erikson, E. H. (1968). *Identity: youth and crisis.* Norton, New York.

Farrell, B. A. (1981). *The standing of psychoanalysis.* Oxford University Press, Oxford.

Feather, N. T. (ed.) (1982). *Expectations and actions: expectancy-value models in psychology.* L. Erlbaum, Hillsdale, NJ.

Field, T. (1978). Interaction behaviors of primary versus secondary caretaker fathers. *Developmental Psychology*, **14**, 183–5.

Fincham, F. and Barling, J. (1978). Locus of control and generosity in learning disabled, normal achieving, and gifted children. *Child Development*, **49**, 530–3.

—— and Jaspars, J. (1979). Attribution of responsibility to the self and others in children and adults. *Journal of Personality and Social Psychology*, **37**, 1589–602.

Findley, M. J. and Cooper, H. M. (1983). Locus of control and academic achievement. *Journal of Personality and Social Psychology*, **44**, 419–27.

Fine, G. A. (1981). Friends, impression management, and preadolescent behavior. In *The development of children's friendships* (eds. S. R. Asher and J. M. Gottman). Cambridge University Press, New York.

Fischer, K. W. (1983). Illuminating the process of moral development. Commentary on Colby, A., Kohlberg, L., Gibbs, J., and Lieberman, M. *Monographs of the Society for Research in Child Development*, **48**, Serial no. 200.

Fiske, S. T. (1981). Social cognition and affect. In *Cognition, social behavior, and the environment* (ed. J. H. Harvey). L. Erlbaum, Hillsdale, NJ.

Fodor, E. M. (1972). Delinquency and susceptability to social influence among adolescents as a function of level of moral judgment. *Journal of Social Psychology*, **86**, 257–60.

Foote, N. N. (1951). Identification as the basis for a theory of motivation. *American Sociological Review*, **16**, 14–31. Reprinted in G. P. Stone and H. A. Faberman (eds.) (1970). *Social psychology through symbolic interaction.* Ginn-Blaisdell, Waltham, Mass.

Ford, M. E. (1979). The construct of egocentrism. *Psychological Bulletin*, **86**, 1169–88.

Francis, R., and Siegal, M. (1984). *Resistance to temptation in children: an attributional analysis*. Paper presented at the Third National Child Development Conference, Perth, Western Australia.

Fraser, C. (1981). The social psychology of unemployment. In *Psychological Survey No. 3* (ed. M. Jeeves). Allen & Unwin, London.

Friend, R. M. and Neale, J. M. (1972). Children's perceptions of success and failure: an attributional analysis of race and social class. *Developmental Psychology*, **7**, 124–8.

Freud, A. (1966). *Normality and pathology of development*. Hogarth Press, London.

Freud, S. (1961a). *Civilization and its discontents: Standard Edition*, *21*. Hogarth Press, London (originally published 1930).

—— (1961b). The ego and the id. In *The complete psychological works of Sigmund Freud. Vol. XIX*. Hogarth Press, London (originally published 1923).

Furman, W. and Masters, J. C. (1980). Peer interactions, sociometric status, and resistance to deviation in young children. *Developmental Psychology*, **16**, 229–36.

Furnham, A. (1982a). Explanations for unemployment in Britain. *European Journal of Social Psychology*, **12**, 335–52.

—— (1982b). Why are the poor always with us: explanations for poverty in Britain. *British Journal of Social Psychology*, **21**, 311–22.

Furth, H. G., Baur, M., and Smith, N. E. (1976). Children's conceptions of social institutions: a Piagetian framework. *Human Development*, **19**, 341–7.

Gallatin, J. (1980). Political thinking in adolescence. In *Handbook of adolescent psychology* (ed. J. Adelson). Wiley, New York.

Garbarino, J. and Crouter, A. (1978). A note on the problem of constant validity in assessing the usefulness of child maltreatment report data. *American Journal of Public Health*, **68**, 598–600.

—— and Sherman, D. (1980). High risk neighborhoods and high risk families: the human ecology of child maltreatment. *Child Development*, **51**, 188–98.

Giarini, O. (1980). *Dialogue on wealth and welfare*. Pergamon Press, Oxford.

—— and Louberge, H. (1978). *The diminishing returns of technology: an essay on the crisis in economic growth*. Pergamon Press, Oxford.

Gil, D. G. (1971). Violence against children. *Journal of Marriage and the Family*, **33**, 637–47.

Gilligan, C. (1982). *In a different voice*. Harvard University Press, Cambridge, Mass.

Giovannoni, J. and Billingsley, A. (1970). Child neglect among the poor: a study of parental inadequacy in families of three ethnic groups. *Child Welfare*, **49**, 196–204.

Gladstone, F. J. (1978). Vandalism among adolescent schoolboys. In *Tackling vandalism* (Home Office Study, No. 47) (ed. R. V. G. Clarke). HMSO, London.

Gnepp, J. (1983). Children's social sensitivity: inferring emotions from conflicting cues. *Developmental Psychology*, **19**, 805–14.

Gold, D. and Andres, D. (1978*a*). Comparisons of adolescent children with employed and nonemployed mothers. *Merrill-Palmer Quarterly*, **24**, 243–54.

—— (1978*b*). Developmental comparisons between ten-year-old children with employed and non-employed mothers. *Child Development*, **49**, 75–84.

Goldberg, D. P. (1972). *The detection of psychiatric illness by questionnaire.* Oxford University Press, Oxford.

Goldschmidt, M. L. T. and Bentler, P. M. (1968). *Concept assessment kit.* San Diego, Educational and Industrial Testing Service.

Gordon, R. A. (1976). Prevalence: the rare datum in delinquency measurement and its implications for the theory of delinquency. In *The juvenile justice system* (ed. M. W. Klein). Sage, Beverly Hills.

Gore, S. (1979). The effect of social support in moderating the health consequences of unemployment. *Journal of Health and Social Behavior*, **19**, 157–65.

Greenberg, D. and Wolf, D. (1982). The economic consequences of experiencing parental marital disruptions. *Children and Youth Services Review*, **4**, 141–62.

Greenberger, E. and Steinberg, L. D. (1983). Sex differences in early labor force experience: harbinger of things to come. *Social Forces*, **62**, 467–86.

—— Steinberg, L. D., Vaux, A., and McAuliffe, S. (1980). Adolescents who work: effects of part-time employment on family and peer relations. *Journal of Youth and Adolescence*, **9**, 189–202.

Greenley, J. R. (1979). Family symptom tolerance and hospitalization experiences of psychiatric patients. In *Research in community and mental health*, Vol. 1 (ed. R. G. Simmons). JAI Press, Greenwich, Conn.

Groenewald, L. P., Tuma, N. B., and Hannan, M. T. (1980). The effects of negative income tax programs on marital dissolution. *Journal of Human Resources*, **15**, 654–74.

Grusec, J. E. and Kuczynski, L. (1980). Direction of effect in socialization: a comparison of the parent's versus the child's behavior as determinants of disciplinary techniques. *Developmental Psychology*, **16**, 1–9.

Gurney, R. M. (1980). The effects of unemployment on the psychological development of school-leavers. *Journal of Occupational Psychology*, **53**, 205–13.

—— (1981). Leaving school, facing unemployment, and making attributions about the causes of unemployment. *Journal of Vocational Behavior*, **18**, 205–13.

—— and Taylor, K. (1981). Research on unemployment: defects, neglect and prospects. *Bulletin of the British Psychological Society*, **34**, 349–52.

Gutek, G., Namamura, C. Y., and Nieva, V. F. (1981). The interdependence of work and family roles. *Journal of Occupational Behavior*, **2**, 1–16.

Haan, N., Langer, J., and Kohlberg, L. (1976). Family patterns of moral reasoning. *Child Development*, **47**, 1204–6.

—— Smith, M. B., and Block, J. (1968). Moral reasoning of young adults: political-social behavior family background, and personality correlates. *Journal of Personality and Social Psychology*, **10**, 183–201.

—— Weiss, R., and Johnson, V. (1982). The role of logic in moral reasoning and development. *Journal of Personality and Social Psychology*, **18**, 245–56.

Hare, R. M. (1952). *The language of morals*. Oxford University Press, Oxford.

Harris, B. (1977). Developmental differences in the attribution of responsibility. *Developmental Psychology*, **13**, 257–65.

Hart, H. L. A. (1968). *Punishment and responsibility: essays in the philosophy of law*. Clarendon Press, Oxford.

Harter, S. (1978). Effectance motivation reconsidered: toward a developmental model. *Human Development*, **21**, 34–64.

—— (1981). A new self-report scale of intrinsic versus extrinsic orientation in the classroom: motivational and informational components. *Developmental Psychology*, **17**, 300–12.

—— (1982a). A cognitive-developmental approach to children's use of affect and trait labels. In *Social cognitive development in context* (ed. F. Serafica). Guildford Press, New York.

—— (1982b). The perceived competence scale for children. *Child Development*, **53**, 87–97.

—— and Barnes, R. (1981). *Children's understanding of parental emotions: a developmental study*. Unpublished manuscript, University of Denver.

—— and Pike, R. (1984). The pictorial scale of perceived competence and social acceptance for young children. *Child Development*, **55**, 1969–82.

Heer, D. M. (1958). Dominance and the working wife. *Social Forces*, **36**, 341–7.

Heider, F. (1958). *The psychology of interpersonal relations*. Wiley, New York.

Henderson, R. W. (1981). Home environment and intellectual performance. In *Parent–child interaction: theory, research, and prospects* (ed. R. W. Henderson). Academic Press, New York.

Henle, M. (1976). Why study the history of psychology. *Annals of the New York Academy of Sciences*, **270**, 14–20.

Henry, R. M. (1980). A theoretical and empirical analysis of 'reasoning' in the socialization of young children. *Human Development*, **23**, 105–25.

Hepworth, S. J. (1980). Moderating factors of the psychological impact of unemployment. *Journal of Occupational Psychology*, **53**, 139–46.

Hess, R. D., Price, G. G., Dickson, W. P., and Conroy, M. (1981). Different roles for mothers and teachers: contrasting styles of child care. *Advances in Early Education and Day Care,* **2,** 1–28.

Hetherington, E. M., Stouwie, R. J., and Ridberg, E. H. (1971). Patterns of family interaction and childrearing related to three dimensions of juvenile delinquency. *Journal of Abnormal Psychology,* **28,** 160–76.

Hinde, R. A., Easton, D. F., Meller, R. E., and Tamplin, A. (1983). Nature and determinants of differential behaviour to adults and peers. *British Journal of Developmental Psychology,* **1,** 3–19.

Hindelang, M. J. (1974). Moral evaluations and illegal behaviors. *Social Problems,* **21,** 370–85.

—— Hirschi, T., and Weis, J. G. (1979). Correlates of delinquency: The illusion of discrepancy between self-report and official measures. *American Sociological Review,* **44,** 995–1014.

Hirschi, T. (1969). *Causes of delinquency.* University of California Press, Berkeley.

Ho, J. and Smithson, M. (1981). *Intergroup attribution amongst unemployed, employed, and school-leaver groups.* Unpublished manuscript, James Cook University of North Queensland.

Hoffman, L. W. (1974). Effects of maternal employment on the child: a review of the research. *Developmental Psychology,* **10,** 204–28.

—— (1977). Changes in family roles, socialization and sex differences. *American Psychologist,* **32,** 644–57.

—— (1979). Maternal employment: 1979. *American Psychologist,* **34,** 859–65.

Hoffman, M. L. (1963). Personality, family structure, and social class as antecedents of parental power assertion. *Child Development,* **34,** 869–84.

—— (1970). Moral development. In *Carmichael's manual of child psychology,* 3rd edition (ed. P. Mussen). Wiley, New York.

—— (1971). Identification and conscience development. *Child Development,* **42,** 1071–82.

—— (1975). Sex differences in moral internalization and values. *Journal of Personality and Social Psychology,* **32,** 720–9.

—— (1977). Sex differences in empathy and related behaviors. *Psychological Bulletin,* **84,** 712–22.

—— and Saltzstein, H. D. (1967). Parent discipline and the child's moral development. *Journal of Personality and Social Psychology,* **5,** 45–57.

Holden, C. (1980). Innovation: Japan races ahead as U.S. falters. *Science,* **210,** 751–4.

Hollingshead, A. B. (1957). *Two factor index of social position.* New Haven, Conn. [Mimeo available from author, Department of Sociology, Yale University.]

Hook, J. G. and Cook, T. D. (1979). Equity theory and the cognitive ability of children. *Psychological Bulletin,* **86,** 429–45.

Houssaidas, L. and Brown, L. B. (1980). Egocentrism in language and space perception: an examination of the concept. *Genetic Psychology Monographs*, **101**, 183–214.

Hsu, F. L. K. (1975). *Iemoto: The Heart of Japan*. Wiley, New York.

Hudgins, W. and Prentice, N. M. (1973). Moral judgment in delinquent and nondelinquent adolescents and their mothers. *Journal of Abnormal Psychology*, **82**, 145–52.

Huston, A. C. (1983). Sex-typing. In *Handbook of child psychology*, 4th edition, Vol. 4 (ed. P. H. Mussen). Wiley, New York.

Inhelder, B., Sinclair, H., and Bovet, M. (1974). *Learning and the development of cognition*. Routledge and Kegan Paul, London.

Irving, K. and Siegal, M. (1983). Mitigating circumstances in children's perceptions of criminal justice: the case of an inability of control events. *British Journal of Developmental Psychology*, **1**, 179–88.

Jahoda, G. (1979). The construction of economic reality by some Glaswegian children. *European Journal of Social Psychology*, **9**, 115–27.

Jahoda, M. (1979). The impact of unemployment in the 1930s and the 1970s. *Bulletin of the British Psychological Society*, **32**, 309–14.

—— (1981). Work, employment, and unemployment: values, theories, and approaches in social research. *American Psychologist*, **36**, 184–91.

Janoff-Bulman, R., and Brickman, P. (1980). Expectations and what people learn from failure. In *Expectancy, incentive and action* (ed. N. T. Feather). L. Erlbaum, Hillsdale, NJ.

Johnson, S. M. and Bolstad, O. P. (1973). Metrodological issues in naturalistic observation: some problems and solutions for field research. In *Behaviour change: Methodology, concepts and practice* (eds. L. A. Hamerlynck, L. C. Handy, and E. J. Mash). Research Press, Champaign, Ill.

Jurkovic, G. J. (1980). The juvenile delinquent as a moral philosopher: a structural-developmental perspective. *Psychological Bulletin*, **88**, 709–27.

—— and Prentice, N. M. (1977). Relation of moral and cognitive development to dimensions of juvenile delinquency. *Journal of Abnormal Psychology*, **86**, 414–20.

Kagan, J. (1958). The concept of identification, *Psychological Review*, **65**, 296–305.

—— (1964). Acquisition and significance of sex typing and sex role identity. In *Review of child development research*, Vol. 1 (eds. M. L. Hoffman and L. W. Hoffman). Russell Sage Foundation, New York.

—— and Lemkin, J. (1960). The child's differential perception of parental attributes. *Journal of Abnormal and Social Psychology*, **61**, 440–7.

—— Hans, S., Markowitz, A., Lopez, D., and Sigal, H. (1982). Validity of children's self-reports of psychological qualities. In *Progress in experimental personality research*, Vol. 11 (eds. B. A. Maher and W. B. Maher). Academic Press, New York.

Karniol R. (1980). A conceptual analysis of immanent justice responses in children. *Child Development*, **51**, 118–30.

—— (1982). Behavioral and cognitive correlates of various immanent justice responses in children: deterent versus punitive moral systems. *Journal of Personality and Social Psychology*, **43**, 811–20.

Keasey, C. B. (1975). Implications of cognitive development for moral reasoning. In *Moral development: current research and theory* (eds. D. J. DePalma and J. M. Foley). L. Erlbaum, Hillsdale, NJ.

Kiefer, C. W. (1970). The psychological interdependence of family, school, and bureaucracy in Japan. *American Anthropologist*, **72**, 66–75.

Kohlberg, L. (1966). A cognitive-developmental analysis of children's sex-role concepts and attitudes. In *The development of sex differences* (ed. E. E. Maccoby). Stanford University Press, Stanford.

—— (1969). Stage and sequence: the cognitive-developmental approach to socialization. In *Handbook of socialization theory and research* (ed. D. A. Goslin). Rand McNally, Chicago.

—— (1976). Moral stages and moral action: the cognitive-developmental approach. In *Moral development and behavior* (ed. T. Lickona). Holt, Rinehart and Winston, New York.

—— (1978). Revisions in the theory and practice of moral development. In *New directions in child development: moral development* (ed. W. Damon). Jossey-Bass, San Francisco.

—— and Kramer, R. B. (1969). Continuities and discontinuities in childhood and adult moral development. *Human Development*, **12**, 93–120.

—— and Turiel, E. (1971). Moral development and moral education. In *Psychology and educational practice* (ed. G. S. Lesser). Scott Foresman, Glenview, Ill.

Kohn, M. L. and Schooler, C. (1978). The reciprocal effects of the substantive complexity of work and intellectual flexibility: a longitudinal assessment. *American Journal of Sociology*, **84**, 24–52.

Kraus, J (1977). Causes of delinquency as perceived by juveniles. *International Journal of Offender Therapy and Comparative Criminology*, **21**, 79–86.

Kraut, R. E. and Lewis, S. H. (1982). Person perception and selfawareness: knowledge of influences on one's own judgments. *Journal of Personality and Social Psychology*, **42**, 448–60.

Krebs, D. and Gillmore, J. (1982). The relationship among the first stages of cognitive development, role-taking, and moral development. *Child Development*, **53**, 877–86.

—— and Rosenwald, A. (1977). Moral reasoning and moral behavior in young adults. *Merrill-Palmer Quarterly*, **23**, 77–87.

Kuhn, D., Langer, J., Kohlberg, L., and Haan, N. (1977). The development of formal operations in logical and moral judgment. *Genetic Psychology Monographs*, **95**, 97–188.

Kurdek, L. A. (1978). Perspective taking as the cognitive basis of children's moral development: a review of the literature. *Merrill-Palmer Quarterly*, **24**, 3–28.

—— (1981). An integrative perspective on children's divorce adjustment. *American Psychologist*, **36**, 856–66.

Kurtines, W. and Greif, E. B. (1974). The development of moral thought: review and evaluation of Kohlberg's approach. *Psychological Bulletin*, **81**, 453–78.

Laosa, L. M. and Brophy, J. E. (1972). Effects of sex and birth order on sex-role development and intelligence among kindergarten children. *Developmental Psychology*, **6**, 409–15.

Langer, J. (1969). Disequilibrium as a source of development. In *Trends and issues in developmental psychology* (eds. P. Mussen, J. Langer, and M. Covington). Holt, Rinehart and Winston, New York.

LaVoie, J. C. (1974). Cognitive determinants of resistance to deviation in seven-, nine-, and eleven-year-old children of low and high maturity of moral judgment. *Developmental Psychology*, **10**, 393–403.

Leahy, R. L. (1983). The development of the conception of economic inequality. II. Explanations, justifications, and conceptions of social mobility and social change. *Developmental Psychology*, **19**, 111–25.

Leibowitz, A. (1977). Parental inputs and children's achievement. *Journal of Human Resources*, **12**, 242–51.

Lenney, E. (1977). Women's self-confidence in achievement settings. *Psychological Bulletin*, **84**, 1–13.

—— and Gold, J. (1982). Sex differences in self-confidence: the effects of task completion and of comparison to competent others. *Personality and Social Psychology Bulletin*, **8**, 74–80.

Lepper, M. R. (1983). Social-control processes and the internalization of social values: an attributional perspective. In *Social cognition and social development: a sociocultural perspective* (eds. E. T. Higgins, D. N. Ruble, and W. W. Hartup). Cambridge University Press, New York.

Lerner, M. (1970). The desire for justice and reactions to victims. In *Altruism and helping behavior* (eds. J. Macaulay and L. Berkowitz). Academic Press, New York.

Lewis, C. C. (1981). The effects of parental firm control: a reinterpretation of findings. *Psychological Bulletin*, **90**, 547–63.

Light, R. (1973). Abused and neglected children in America: a study of alternative policies. *Harvard Educational Review*, **43**, 556–98.

Liker, J. K. and Elder, G. H., Jr. (1983). Economic hardship and marital relations in the 1930s. *American Sociological Review*, **48**, 343–59.

Loeber, R. and Dishion, T. (1983). Early predictors of male delinquency: a review. *Psychological Bulletin*, **94**, 68–99.

Lynn, R. (1982). National differences in anxiety and extroversion. In *Progress in experimental personality research*, Vol. 11 (eds. B. A. Maher and W. B. Maher). Academic Press, New York.

Lyons, N. P. (1983). Two perspectives: on self, relationships, and morality. *Harvard Educational Review*, **53**, 125–45.

Macarov, D. (1982). *Worker productivity: myths and reality*. Sage, Beverly Hills.

McClelland, D. C. (1975). *Power: the inner experience*. Irvington, New York.

McClelland, D. C. and Pilon, D. A. (1983). Sources of adult motives in patterns of parent behavior in early childhood. *Journal of Personality and Social Psychology*, **44**, 564–74.

Maccoby, E. E. and Jacklin, C. N. (1974). *The psychology of sex differences*. Stanford University Press, Stanford.

McCord, J. (1979). Some childrearing antecedents of criminal behavior in adult men. *Journal of Personality and Social Psychology*, **37**, 1477–86.

—— McCord, J., and Thurber, E. (1963). Effects of maternal employment on lower-class boys. *Journal of Abnormal and Social Psychology*, **67**, 177–82.

McCrae, R. R. and Costa, P. T., Jr. (1982). Self-concept and the stability of personality: cross-sectional comparisons. *Journal of Personality and Social Psychology*, **43**, 1282–92.

Macfarlane, J. W., Allen, L., and Honzik, M. P. (1954). *A developmental study of the behavior problems of normal children between twenty-one months and fourteen years*. University of California Press, Berkeley.

McGarvey, B., Gabrielli, W. F., Jr., Bentler, P. M., and Mednick, S. A. (1981). Rearing social class, education, and criminality: a multiple indicator model. *Journal of Abnormal Psychology*, **90**, 354–64.

McGuire, W. J. and McGuire, C. V. (1982). Significant others in self-space: sex differences and developmental trends in the social self. In *Psychological perspectives on the self*, Vol. 1 (ed. J. Suls). L. Erlbaum, Hillsdale, NJ.

Mackenzie, B. (1984). Explaining race differences in IQ: the logic, the methodology, and the evidence. *American Psychologist*, **39**, 1214–33.

Maehr, M. L. (1974). *Sociocultural origins of achievement*. Wadsworth, Belmont, Cal.

Mancuso, J. C. and Allen, D. A. (1976). Children's perceptions of a transgressor's socialization as a function of type of reprimand. *Human Development*, **19**, 277–90.

Masterson, J. F. (1968). The psychiatric significance of adolescent turmoil. *American Journal of Psychiatry*, **127**, 1549–54.

Mischel, W. (1968). *Personality and assessment*. Wiley, New York.

—— Zeiss, R., and Zeiss, A. (1974). Internal-external control and persistance: validation and implications of the Stanford Preschool Internal-External scale. *Journal of Personality and Social Psychology*, **29**, 265–78.

Moffitt, T. E., Gabrielli, W. F., Mednick, S. A., and Schulsinger, F. (1981). Socioeconomic status, IQ, and delinquency. *Journal of Abnormal Psychology*, **90**, 152–6.

Moore, T. (1975). Exclusive early mothering and its alternatives: the outcome of adolescence. *Scandinavian Journal of Psychology*, **16**, 255–72.

Morse, S. J. (1979). Diminished capacity: a moral and legal conundrum. *International Journal of Law and Psychiatry*, **2**, 271–98.

Mortimer, J. T. and Lorence, J. (1979). Occupational experience and the self-concept: a longitudinal study. *Social Psychology Quarterly*, **42**, 307–23.

Mowrer, O. H. (1950). *Learning theory and personality dynamics*. Ronald Press, New York.

—— (1953). Neurosis and psychotherapy as interpersonal process: a synopsis. In *Psychotherapy: theory and research* (ed. O. H. Mowrer). Ronald Press, New York.

Mussen, P., Harris, S., Rutherford, E., and Keasey, C. B. (1970). Honesty and altruism among preadolescents. *Developmental Psychology*, **3**, 169–94.

Nelson, S. A. and Dweck, C. S. (1977). Motivation and competence as determinants of young children's reward allocation. *Developmental Psychology*, **13**, 192–7.

Nisbett, R. E. and Wilson, T. D. (1977). Telling more than we can know: verbal reports on mental processes. *Psychological Review*, **84**, 231–59.

Nixon, J., Pearn, J., Wilkey, I., and Petrie, G. (1981). Social class and violent child death: an analysis of fatal nonaccidental injury, murder, and fatal child neglect. *Child Abuse and Neglect*, **5**, 111–16.

Norman-Jackson, J. (1982). Family interactions, language development, and primary reading achievement of black children in families of low income. *Child Development*, **53**, 349–58.

Nowicki, S. and Duke, M. P. (1974). A preschool and primary internal–external control scale. *Developmental Psychology*, **10**, 874–80.

—— and Duke, M. (1979). Preschool and primary locus of control: a reply. *Developmental Psychology*, **15**, 325–8.

—— and Segal, W. (1974). Perceived parental characteristics, locus of control orientation, and behavioral correlates of locus of control. *Developmental Psychology*, **10**, 33–7.

—— and Strickland, B. R. (1973). A locus of control scale for children. *Journal of Consulting and Clinical Psychology*, **40**, 148–55.

Nucci, L. (1981). Conceptions of personal issues: a domain distinct from moral or societal concepts. *Child Development*, **52**, 114–21.

—— and Herman, S. (1982). Behaviorally disordered children's conceptions of moral, conventional, and personal issues. *Journal of Abnormal Child Psychology*, **10**, 411–26.

—— and Nucci, M. S. (1982). Children's social interactions in the context of moral and conventional trangressions. *Child Development*, **53**, 403–12.

—— and Turiel, E. (1978). Social interactions and the development of social concepts in preschool children. *Child Development*, **49**, 400–7.

Odagiri, H. (1982). Antineoclassical management motivation in a neoclassical economy: a model of economic growth and Japan's experience. *Kyklos*, **35**, 223–43.

Osman, L. M. (1982). Conformity on compliance? A study of sex differences in pedestrian behavior. *British Journal of Social Psychology*, **21**, 19–21.

Parke, R. D. (1979). Perspectives on father–infant interaction. In *Handbook of infant development* (ed. J. D. Osofsky). Wiley, New York.

—— (1981). *Fathering*. Fontana, Glasgow.

Parke, R. D., Power, T. G., and Gottman, J. M. (1979). Conceptualizing and quantifying influence patterns in the family triad. In *The study of social interaction: methodological issues* (eds. M. E. Lamb, S. J. Suomi, and G. R. Stephenson). University of Wisconsin Press, Madison.

Parsons, J. E., Adler, T. F., and Kaczala, C. M. (1982). Socialization of achievement attitudes and beliefs: parental influences. *Child Development*, **53**, 310–21.

Parsons, T. and Bales, T. F. (1955). *Family, socialization, and interaction process*. Free Press, Glencoe, Ill.

Patterson, G. R. (1981). Some speculations and data relating to children who steal. In *Theory and fact in contemporary criminology* (eds. T. Hirschi and M. Gottfredson). Sage, Beverly Hills.

Peele, S. (1981). Reductionism in the psychology of the eighties: can biochemistry eliminate addiction, mental illness and pain? *American Psychologist*, **36**, 807–18.

Pelton, L. H. (1978). Child abuse and neglect: the myth of classlessness. *American Journal of Orthopsychiatry*, **48**, 609–17.

Perret-Clermont, A.-N. (1980). *Social interaction and cognitive development in children*. Academic Press, London.

Perry, D. G. and Perry, L. C. (1983). Social learning, causal attribution, and moral internalization. In *Learning in children: progress in cognitive development research* (eds. J. Bisanz, G. L. Bisanz, and R. Kail). Springer-Verlag, New York.

Piaget, J. (1977a). *The development of thought: equilibration of cognitive structures*. Blackwell, Oxford.

—— (1977b). *The moral judgement of the child*. Penguin, Harmondsworth (originally published by Routledge and Kegan Paul, London, 1932).

Prior, J. B. (1980). Self-reports and behavior. In *The self in social psychology* (eds. D. M. Wegner and R. K. Vallacher). Oxford University Press, New York.

Propper, A. M. (1972). The relationship of maternal employment to adolescent roles, activities, and parental relationships. *Journal of Marriage and the Family*, **34**, 417–21.

Putnam, H. (1973). Reductionism and the nature of psychology. *Cognition*, **2**, 479–502.

Radin, N. (1972). Father–child interaction and the intellectual functioning of four-year-old boys. *Developmental Psychology*, **6**, 353–61.

—— (1973). Observed paternal behaviors as antecedents of intellectual functioning in young boys. *Developmental Psychology*, **8**, 369–76.

Renshaw, J. R. (1976). An exploration of the dynamics of the overlapping worlds of work and family. *Family Process*, **15**, 143–65.

Rest, J. (1983). Morality. In *Handbook of child psychology*, Vol. 3 (eds. J. H. Flavell and E. Markman). Wiley, New York.

Richman, L. C. and Harper, D. C. (1979). Parental childrearing characteristics and delinquent adolescents' response to behavioral treatment. *American Journal of Orthopsychiatry*, **18**, 527–9.

Robinson, J. (1968). *Essays in the theory of economic growth*. Macmillan, London.

Rockwell, R. C. and Elder, G. H., Jr. (1982). Economic deprivation in children's problem behavior. *Human Development*, **25**, 57–64.

Rohlen, T. P. (1974). *For harmony and strength: Japanese white collar organization in anthropological perspective*. University of California Press, Berkeley.

Rose, D. J., Boughman, J. A., Corey, L. A., Nance, W. E., Christian, J. C., and Kang, K. W. (1980). Data from kinships of monozygotic twins indicate maternal effects on verbal intelligence. *Nature*, **283**, 357–77.

Ross, H. L. and Sawhill, I. V. (1975). *Time of transition: the growth of families headed by women*. Urban Institute, Washington.

Rothbaum, F., Weisz, J. R., and Snyder, S. S. (1982). Changing the world and changing the self: a two-process model of perceived control. *Journal of Personality and Social Psychology*, **42**, 5–37.

Rubenstein, J. L., Howes, C., and Boyle, P. (1981). A two-year follow-up of infants in community-based daycare. *Journal of Child Psychology and Psychiatry*, **22**, 209–18.

Rubin, K. H. (1978). Role-taking in childhood: some methodological considerations. *Child Development*, **49**, 428–33.

—— and Trotter, K. T. (1977). Kohlberg's moral judgment scale: some methodological considerations. *Developmental Psychology*, **13**, 535–6.

Ruble, D. N., Boggiano, A. K., Feldman, N. S., and Loebl, J. H. (1980). Developmental analysis of the role of social comparison in self-evaluation. *Developmental Psychology*, **16**, 105–15.

Russell, G. (1978). The father role and its relation to masculinity, femininity, and androgyny. *Child Development*, **48**, 1174–81.

—— (1982). Shared-caregiving families: an Australian sample. In *Nontraditional families: Parenting and child development* (ed. M. E. Lamb). L. Erlbaum, Hillsdale, NJ.

Russell, J. (1978). *The acquisition of knowledge*. Macmillan, London.

—— (1981). Dyadic interaction in a logical reasoning problem requiring inclusion ability. *Child Development*, **52**, 1322–5.

Rutter, M. and Giller, H. (1983). *Juvenile delinquency: trends and perspectives*. Penguin, Harmondsworth.

Ryle, G. (1949). *The concept of mind*. Hutchinson, London.

Sagi, A. (1982). Antecedents and consequences of various degrees of paternal involvement in child rearing: the Israeli project. In *Nontraditional families: parenting and child development* (ed. M. E. Lamb). L. Erlbaum, Hillsdale, NJ.

Salili, F., Maehr, M. L., and Gillmore, G. (1976). Achievement and morality: a cross-cultural analysis of causal attribution and evaluation. *Journal of Personality and Social Psychology*, **33**, 327–37.

Saltzstein, H. D. (1983). Critical issues in Kohlberg's theory of moral reasoning. Commentary on Colby, A., Kohlberg, L., Gibbs, J., and

Lieberman, M. *Monographs of the Society for Research in Child Development*, **48**, Serial no. 200.

Sampson, E. E. (1981). Cognitive psychology as ideology. *American Psychologist*, **36**, 730–43.

Sandler, I. N. and Block, M. (1979). Life stress and maladaptation of children. *American Journal of Community Psychology*, **7**, 425–40.

Sanford, N. (1955). The dynamics of identification. *Psychological Review*, **62**, 106–18.

Santrock, J. W. (1975). Moral structure: the interrelations of moral behavior, moral judgment, and moral affect. *Journal of Genetic Psychology*, **127**, 201–13.

—— and Warshak, R. A. (1979). Father custody and social development in boys and girls. *Journal of Social Issues*, **35**, 112–25.

—— Warshak, R., Lindbergh, C., and Meadows, L. (1982). Children's and parents' observed social behavior in stepfather families. *Child Development*, **53**, 472–80.

Sasaki, N. (1981). *Management and industrial structure in Japan*. Pergamon, Oxford.

Scarse, R. (1974). Relative deprivation: a comparison of English and Swedish manual workers. In *Poverty, inequality and class structure* (ed. D. Wedderburn). Cambridge University Press, Cambridge.

Schaefer, E. S. (1965*a*). Children's reports of parental behavior: an inventory. *Child Development*, **36**, 413–24.

—— (1965*b*). A configurational analysis of children's reports of parental behavior. *Journal of Consulting Psychology*, **29**, 552–7.

Scheck, D. C. and Emerick, R. (1976). The young male adolescent's perception of early childrearing behavior: the differential effects of socioeconomic status and family size. *Sociometry*, **39**, 39–52.

Schneider, D. J., Hastorf, A. H., and Ellsworth, P. C. (1979). *Person perception* (2nd edition). Addison-Wesley, Reading, Mass.

Schwartz, S. and Johnson, J. H. (1981). *Psychopathology of childhood: a clinical-experimental approach*. Pergamon, New York.

Schwarz, J. C., Krolick, G., and Strickland, R. G. (1973). Effects of early daycare experience on adjustment to a new environment. *American Journal of Orthopsychiatry*, **43**, 340–6.

Sears, R. R. (1957). Identification as a form of behavioral development. In *The concept of development* (ed. D. B. Harris). University of Minnesota Press, Minneapolis.

Selman, R. L. (1980). *The growth of interpersonal understanding*. Academic Press, New York.

Semin, G. R. (1980). A gloss on attribution theory. *British Journal of Social and Clinical Psychology*, **19**, 291–300.

Shapland, J. (1981). *Between conviction and sentence: the process of mitigation*. Routledge and Kegan Paul, London.

Shepherd, G. (1981). Psychological disorder and unemployment. *Bulletin of the British Psychological Society*, **34**, 345–8.

Shevrin, H. and Dickman, S. (1980). The psychological unconscious: a necessary assumption for all psychological theory? *American Psychologist*, **35**, 421–34.

Shore, M. F. and Massimo, J. L. (1979). Fifteen years after treatment: a followup of comprehensive vocationally-oriented psychotherapy. *American Journal of Orthopsychiatry*, **49**, 240–5.

Shweder, R. A. (1982). Beyond self-constructed knowledge: the study of culture and morality. *Merrill-Palmer Quarterly*, **28**, 41–69.

Siegal, M. (1981). Children's perceptions of adult economic needs. *Child Development*, **52**, 379–83.

—— (1982). *Fairness in children: a social-cognitive approach to the study of moral development*. Academic Press, London.

—— (1984*a*). Diminished responsibility as a mitigating circumstance in juvenile offenders' legal judgments. *Journal of Adolescence*, **7**, 233–44.

—— (1984*b*). Social cognition and the development of rule-guided behaviour. *Australian Journal of Psychology*, **36**, 387–98.

—— and Cowen, J. (1984). Appraisals of intervention: the mother's versus the culprit's behavior as determinants of children's evaluations of discipline techniques. *Child Development*, **55**, 1760–6.

—— and Francis, R. (1982). Parent–child relations and cognitive approaches to the development of moral judgement and behaviour. *British Journal of Psychology*, **73**, 285–94.

—— and Rablin, J. (1982). Moral development as reflected by young children's evaluations of maternal discipline. *Merrill-Palmer Quarterly*, **28**, 499–509.

—— and Shwalb, D. W. (in press). Economic justice in adolescence: an Australian–Japanese comparison. *Journal of Economic Psychology*.

—— and Storey, R. M. (in press). Daycare and children's conceptions of moral and social rules. *Child Development*, **56**.

Simmons, A. G., Rosenberg, F., and Rosenberg, M. (1973). Disturbance in the self image at adolescence. *American Sociological Review*, **38**, 553–68.

Simons, R. L. (1978). The meaning of the IQ–delinquency relationship. *American Sociological Review*, **43**, 268–70.

Skeen, J. A. and Gelfand, D. M. (1981). *Children's perceptions of their mothers and fathers*. Paper presented at the Annual Meeting of the Western Psychological Association, Los Angeles.

Slater, P. E. (1961). Toward a dualistic theory of identification. *Merrill-Palmer Quarterly*, **7**, 113–26.

Smetana, J. G. (1981). Preschool children's conceptions of moral and social rules. *Child Development*, **52**, 1333–6.

—— (1983). *Adults' and toddlers' responses to moral and conventional transgressions*. Paper presented at the Biennial Meetings of the Society for Research in Child Development, Detroit.

—— (1984). Morality and gender: a commentary on Pratt, Golding, and Hunter. *Merrill-Palmer Quarterly*, **30**, 341–8.

Smetana, J. G., Kelly, M., and Twentyman, C. T. (1984). Abused, neglected, and nonmaltreated children's conceptions of moral and social-conventional transgressions. *Child Development*, **55**, 277–87.

Smith, E. R. and Kluegel, J. R. (1982). Cognitive and social bases of emotional experience: outcome, attribution, and affect. *Journal of Personality and Social Psychology*, **43**, 1129–41.

Snow, M. E., Jacklin, C. N., and Maccoby, E. E. (1981). Birth-order differences in peer sociability at thirty-three months. *Child Development*, **52**, 589–95.

Sohn, D. (1982). Sex differences in achievement self-attributions: an effect–size analysis. *Sex Roles*, **8**, 345–57.

Spenner, K. I. and Featherman, D. L. (1978). Achievement ambitions. In *Annual Review of Sociology*, Vol. 4 (eds. R. Turner, J. S. Coleman, and R. Fox). Reviews, Palo Alto, Cal.

Spivack, G. (1957). Childrearing attitudes of emotionally disturbed adolescents. *Journal of Consulting Psychology*, **21**, 178.

Staub, E. (1979). *Positive social behavior and morality, Vol. 2: Socialization and development*. Academic Press, New York.

Stein, A. H. and Bailey, M. M. (1973). The socialization of achievement orientation in females. *Psychological Bulletin*, **80**, 345–66.

Steinberg, L. D. and Greenberger, L. D. (1980). The part-time employment of high school students: a research agenda. *Children and Youth Services Review*, **2**, 159–83.

—— Catalano, R., and Dooley, D. (1981). Economic antecedents of child abuse and neglect. *Child Development*, **52**, 975–85.

—— Greenberger, E., Jacobi, M., and Garduque, L. (1981). Early work experience: a partial antidote for adolescent egocentrism. *Journal of Youth and Adolescence*, **10**, 141–57.

—— Greenberger, E., Garduque, L., Ruggiero, M., and Vaux, A. (1982) The effects of working on adolescent development. *Developmental Psychology*, **18**, 385–95.

Stoke, S. M. (1950). An inquiry into the concept of identification. *Journal of Genetic Psychology*, **76**, 163–89. (Reprinted in 1954, *Readings in child development* (eds. W. E. Martin and C. B. Stendler). Harcourt, Brace and Company, New York.)

Straker, G. and Jacobson, R. S. (1981). Aggression, emotional maladjustment, and empathy in the abused child. *Developmental Psychology*, **17**, 762–65.

Sutherland, E. H. and Cressey, D. R. (1974). *Principles of criminology*. Lippincott, Philadelphia (originally published 1939).

Tapp, J. L. and Kohlberg, L. (1977). Developing senses of law and legal justice. In *Law, justice, and the individual in society* (eds. J. L. Tapp and F. J. Levine). Holt, Rinehart and Winston, New York.

Tesser, A. (1980). Self-esteem maintenance in family dynamics. *Journal of Personality and Social Psychology*, **39**, 77–91.

Tisak, M. S. and Ford, M. E. (1983). *Children's conceptions of moral and prosocial events: further distinctions in social-cognitive development.* Paper presented at the Biennial Meetings of the Society for Research in Child Development, Detroit.

Tittle, C. R., Villemez, W. J., and Smith D. A. (1978). The myth of social class and criminality: an empirical assessment of the empirical evidence. *American Sociological Review*, **43**, 643–56.

Tsurumi, Y. (1978). *Japanese business: A research guide with annotated bibliography.* Praeger, New York.

Turiel, E. (1966). An experimental test of the sequentiality of developmental stages in the child's moral judgement. *Journal of Personality and Social Psychology*, **3**, 611–18.

—— (1978). Distinct conceptual and developmental domains: social-convention and morality. In *Nebraska Symposium on Motivation*, Vol. 25 (ed. C. B. Keasey). University of Nebraska Press, Lincoln.

—— (1983a). *The development of social knowledge: morality and convention.* Cambridge University Press, New York.

—— (1983b). Domains and categories in social cognitive development. In *The relationship between social and cognitive development* (ed. W. Overton). L. Erlbaum, Hillsdale, NJ.

Tygart, C. E. (1982). Effects of religiosity on public opinion about legal responsibility for mentally retarded fellows. *American Journal of Mental Deficiency*, **86**, 459–64.

Underwood, B. and Moore, B. (1982). Perspective-taking and altruism. *Psychological Bulletin*, **91**, 143–73.

US Department of Commerce, Bureau of the Census. (1979). *Population profile of the United States: 1978, population characteristics.* (Current Population Reports, Series P-20, No. 336.) US Government Printing Office, Washington, DC.

Van Dijk, J. J. M. and Steinmetz, C. H. D. (1982). *Beyond measuring the volume of crime.* Ministry of Justice, The Hague, Netherlands.

Vogel, D. (1981). My childhood cities. In *The Penguin book of Hebrew verse* (ed. T. Carmi). Penguin, Harmondsworth.

Wagar, J. A. (1970). Growth versus the quality of life. *Science*, **168**, 1179–84.

Walker, N. D. (1977). *Behaviour and misbehaviour: explanations and non-explanations.* Blackwell, Oxford.

Warr, P. and Parry, G. (1982). Paid employment and women's psychological well-being. *Psychological Bulletin*, **91**, 498–516.

Watson, M. M. and Amgott-Kwan, T. (1983). Development of family role concepts in school-age children. *Developmental Psychology*, **19**, 659–66.

Wayman, T. (1973). *Waiting for Wayman.* McClelland and Stewart, Toronto.

Weiner, B. (1980). *Human motivation.* Holt, Rinehart and Winston, New York.

—— and Kukla, A. (1970). An attributional analysis of achievement motivation. *Journal of Personality and Social Psychology*, **15**, 1–20.

Weiner, B. and Peter, N. (1973). A cognitive-developmental analysis of achievement and moral judgments. *Developmental Psychology*, **9**, 290–309.

—— Graham, S., Stern, P., and Lawson, M. E. (1982). Using affective cues to infer causal thoughts. *Developmental Psychology*, **18**, 278–86.

Weiner, I. B. (1970). *Psychological disturbance in adolescence*. Wiley-Interscience, New York.

Weisz, J. R. (1980). Autonomy, control, and other reasons why 'Mom is the Greatest': a content analysis of children's Mother's Day letters. *Child Development*, **51**, 801–7.

West, D. J. (1982). *Delinquency: its roots, careers, and prospects*. Heinemann, London.

Weston, D. and Turiel, E. (1980). Act-rule relations: children's concepts of social rules. *Developmental Psychology*, **116**, 417–24.

Wheaton, B. (1980). The sociogenesis of psychological disorder: an attributional theory. *Journal of Health and Social Behavior*, **21**, 100–24.

White, K. R. (1982). The relation between socioeconomic status and academic achievement. *Psychological Bulletin*, **91**, 461–81.

White, P. (1980) Limitations on verbal reports of internal events: a refutation of Nisbett and Wilson and of Bem. *Psychological Review*, **87**, 105–12.

White, R. W. (1959). Motivation reconsidered: the concept of competence. *Psychological Review*, **66**, 297–333.

Whitehill, A. M. and Takezawa, S. (1968). *The other worker*. East West Center Press, Honolulu.

Whiteman, M. (1979). The role of intention in subjective and objective responsibility. In *Cognitive growth and development: essays in memory of Herbert G. Birch* (ed. M. Bortner). Brunner/Mazel, New York.

Wichern, F. and Nowicki, S. (1976). Independence training practices and locus of control orientation in children and adolescents. *Developmental Psychology*, **12**, 77.

Willerman, L. (1979). Effects of families on intellectual development. *American Psychologist*, **34**, 923–9.

Wilson, H. (1980). Parental supervision: a neglected aspect of delinquency. *British Journal of Criminology*, **20**, 203–35.

Winer, B. J. (1970). *Statistical principles in experimental design*. McGraw-Hill, New York.

Winocur, S. and Siegal, M. (1982). Adolescents' judgements of economic arrangements. *International Journal of Behavioral Development*, **5**, 351–65.

Yarrow, M. R. and Waxler, C. Z. (1979). The analysis of social interactions. In *The analysis of social interactions: methods, issues, and illustrations* (ed. R. B. Cairns). L. Erlbaum, Hillsdale, NJ.

Yussen, S. (1977). Characteristics of moral dilemmas written by adolescents. *Developmental Psychology*, **13**, 162–3.

Zahn-Waxler, C., Radke-Yarrow, M., and King, R. A. (1979). Childrearing and children's prosocial initiations toward victims of distress. *Child Development*, **50**, 319–30.

Zajonc, R. B. (1984). On the primacy of affect. *American Psychologist*, **39**, 117–23.

Zawadski, B. and Lazarsfeld, P. (1935). The psychological consequences of unemployment. *Journal of Social Psychology*, **6**, 224–51.

Zelkowitz, P., Saunders, E., Longfellow, C., and Belle, D. (1979). *Stress and depression: their impact on the mother–child relationship*. Paper presented at the Biennial Meetings of the Society for Research in Child Development, San Francisco.

Author Index

Aberle, D. F. 16
Acock, A. C. 1
Adams, J. 100
Adelson, J. 51, 88
Adler, A. 121
Adler, T. F. 48–51
Allen, D. A. 65
Allen, L. 7
Allport, G. 126
Amgott-Kwan, T. 115
Andres, D. 129–30
Andrews, R. J. 37
Appel, Y. H. 60–3
Armentrout, J. A. 67
Atwood, M. 124

Babad, E. Y. 34
Bahr, S. J. 129
Bailey, M. M. 51
Baldus, B. 98
Baldwin, J. M. 32, 61, 81, 96
Dales, T. F. 98
Bandura, A. 20, 25, 70
Banks, M. H. 12
Barahal, R. M. 133
Barling, J. 55
Barnes, R. 115–16
Bauer, P. T. 4
Baumrind, D. 43, 59, 65, 105
Baur, M. 98
Becker, G. S. 10, 134
Beecher, W. 121
Beeghly, M. 61
Bell, R. Q. 70
Belle, D. 13
Belsky, J. 17, 74, 136
Bem, D. 32
Bem, S. L. 105
Bengston, V. L. 1
Bentler, P. M. 36
Berg-Cross, L. G. 85

Bettleheim, B. 22
Bhrolchain, M. N. 12
Bierman, K. L. 82
Billingsley, A. 13
Bixenstine, B. A. 29
Bixenstine, V. E. 29
Black, A. 76, 78
Blasi, A. 19, 29
Blatt, M. M. 28
Block, J. 122, 131
Block, J. H. 41, 131
Block, M. 12
Bolstad, O. D. 34, 43
Boucher, J. 61
Bovet, M. 112
Bowerman, C. E., 129
Boyle, P. 74, 80
Bradley, R. H. 53
Brandwein, R. A. 134
Bretherton, I. 61
Brickman, P. 91
Brislin, R. W. 108
Bronfenbrenner, U. 4–5, 16, 24–5, 126
Brophy, J. E. 42
Broughton, J. M. 32
Brown, C. A. 134
Brown, G. W. 12
Brown, L. B. 19, 85
Brown, M. 2, 100
Bryant, P. E. 113–14
Burger, G. K. 67
Burger, J. M. 48
Bussey, K 30

Caldwell, B. M. 53
Campbell, A. 11
Candee, D. 19, 31, 123
Carey, P. 83
Catalano, R. 12, 14
Caudill, W. A. 110

Chandler, T. A. 56
Chodorow, N. 30, 35, 41–2
Clarke, R. V. G. 83
Clingempeel, W. G. 131
Cohn, A. 87
Coie, J. D. 81
Colby, A. 19, 28–30
Cole, R. E. 106
Connell, R. W. 98–9, 106
Conroy, M. 110
Converse, P. E. 11
Cook, T. D. 3, 101, 133, 136
Cooper, H. M. 48, 56
Coppetelli, H. 81
Cortese, A. J. 29
Costa, P. T. 123
Covington, M. V. 57
Cowen, J. C. 64, 68, 70
Crandall, V. C. 48, 55
Crandall, V. J. 48, 55
Cressey, D. R. 8
Crouter, A. 14

Dalenberg, C. J. 82
Damon, W. 28, 101, 114–17
Danziger, K. 34
Darley, J. M. 85, 87
Davidson, P. 76, 78
Davies, D. B. 1
Davies, M. 52
Deaux, K. 57
DeCorte, M. S. 29
Derber, C. 5
DeVos, G. 110
Dickman, S. 20
Dienstbier, R. A. 28
Dishion, T. 93
Dix, T. 59, 82
Dodge, K. A. 81
Dooley, D. 12, 14
Douvan, E. 51, 128
Duke, M. P. 55
Dusek, J. B. 122–3
Dweck, C. S. 46–8, 100
Dworkin, R. 133

Eccles, J. 49, 51, 53
Eekelaar, J. 136
Eisenberg, N. 30
Eisenberg, P. 6, 136

Elardo, R. 53
Elder, G. H. 7, 10, 127, 136
Elkind, D. 28
Elkins, J. 37
Ellsworth, P. C. 57
Emerick, R. 1, 9
Emprey, L. T. 8
Endler, N. S. 70
Enright, R. D. 101–2
Enright, W. F. 101–2
Epstein, S. 43
Erikson, E. 11, 122

Farrell, B. A. 22, 31
Feather, N. T. 57
Featherman, D. L. 52
Field, T. 131
Fincham, F. 55, 85
Findley, M. J. 56
Fine, G. A. 32
Fischer, K. W. 29
Fiske, S. T. 20
Flaherty, J. F. 122–3
Fodor, E. M. 90
Foote, N. N. 22–3
Ford, M. E. 19, 77, 80
Fox, E. M. 134
Francis, R. 35, 41
Fraser, C. 136
Freud, A. 122
Freud, S. 21–6, 31, 120
Friend, R. M. 46
Furman, W. 81–2
Furnham, A. 100
Furth, H. G. 98

Gallatin, J. 107
Garbarino, J. 12, 14
Gelfand, D. M. 60
Giarini, O. 2
Gil, D. G. 13, 14
Giller, H. 30, 96
Gilligan, C. 30, 35, 39, 42
Gillmore, G. 99
Gillmore, J. 27
Giovannoni, J. 13
Gladstone, F. J. 94–5
Gnepp, J. 118
Gold, D. 129–30
Gold, J. 52

Goldberg, D. P. 12
Goldschmidt, M. L. T. 36
Good, T. L. 48
Goodman, E. 2
Gordon, R. A. 8
Gore, S. 132
Gottman, J. M. 10
Green, B. 88
Greenberg, D. 134
Greenberger, E. 134-5
Greenley, J. R. 6
Greif, E. B. 28
Groenewald, L. P. 134
Grusec, J. E. 59, 66, 82
Gurney, R. M. 11, 100, 135
Gutek, G. 110

Haan, N. 26-7, 122
Hannan, M. T. 134
Hare, R. M. 124
Harper, L. 70
Harris, B. 85
Harris, T. 12
Hart, H. L. A. 84
Harter, S. 55-6, 115-7
Hastorf, A. H. 57
Heer, D. M. 129
Heider, F. 45-6, 85, 87, 105
Henderson, R. W. 53-4
Henle, M. 44
Henry, R. M. 65
Hepworth, S. J. 12
Herman, S. 90-3
Hess, R. D. 80
Hinde, R. A. 42
Hindelang, M. J. 8-9, 83
Hirschi, T. 8-9
Ho, J. 99
Hoffman, L. W. 127-8, 134
Hoffman, M. L. 30, 33-6, 64, 66, 69, 82,
    103, 131
Holden, C. 106
Honzik, M. P. 7
Hook, J. G. 101
Houssaidas, L. 19
Howes, C. 74, 80
Hsu, F. L. K. 106
Hudgins, W. 90
Hunt, J. McV. 70
Huston, A. C. 30

Inbar, J. 34
Inhelder, B. 112
Irving, K. 87

Jacklin, C. N. 42, 98
Jackson, P. R. 12
Jacobson, R. S. 133
Jahoda, G. 98
Jahoda, M. 11, 136
Janoff-Bulman, R. 91
Jaspars, J. 85
Johnson, J. H. 10
Johnson, S. M. 34, 43
Johnson, V. 27
Jurkovic, G. J. 19, 84, 90

Kaczala, C. M. 48-51
Kagan, J. 23-6, 32, 56, 70
Kandel, D. B. 1, 52
Karniol, R. 34, 120-1
Katkovsky, W. 48, 55
Keasey, C. B. 27
Kelly, M. 74, 78
Kiefer, C. W. 110
Killen, M. 28, 114
King, R. A. 65, 69
Klosson, E. C. 85, 87
Kluegel, J. R. 11
Kohlberg, L. 18-20, 25-31, 40-1, 43,
    90-1, 113, 122-3
Kuhn, M. 11
Kramer, R. B. 122
Kraus, J. 93
Kraut, R. E. 33
Krebs, D. 20, 27
Krolick, G. 74
Kuczynski, L. 66
Kuhn, D. 27
Kukla, A. 46
Kurdek, L. A. 19, 131
Kurtines, W. 28

Lallijee, M. 85
Landes, E. M. 10, 134
Langer, J. 26, 114-15
Laosa, L. M. 42
Lapsley, D. K. 101-2
LaVoie, J. C. 65
Lazarsfeld, P. 6, 136
Leahy, R. L. 98

Leibowitz, A. 54
Lemkin, J. 70
Lenney, E. 52
Lennon, R. 30
Lepper, M. 59
Lerner, M. 105
Lewis, C. C. 59
Lewis, S. H. 33
Light, R. 14
Liker, J. K. 7
Loeber, R. 93
Lorence, J. 11
Louberge, H. 2
Lynn, R. 111
Lyons, N. P. 30, 32

Macarov, D. 106
McClelland, D. C. 104–5
Maccoby, E. E. 42, 98
McCord, J. 8–9, 93, 128
McCrae, R. R. 123
Macfarlane, J. W. 7
McGarvey, B. 9
McGuire, C. V. 26
McGuire, W. J. 26
Mackenzie, B. 54
Madge, N. 2, 100
Maehr, M. L. 45, 99
Mancuso, J. C. 65
Martin, H. P. 133
Massimo, J. L. 135
Masters, J. C. 81
Masterson, J. F. 123
Maughan, B. 30
Meece, J. L. 49, 51
Michael, R. T. 10, 134
Mischel, W. 55, 71
Moffitt, T. E. 10
Moore, B. 19
Moore, T. 74
Morrison, A. 131
Morse, S. J. 85
Mortimer, J. T. 11
Mowrer, O. H. 23–5
Museen, P. 34–5

Naegele, K. D. 16
Namamura, C. Y. 110
Neale, J. M. 46
Nelson, S. A. 100

Nieva, V. F. 110
Nisbett, R. E. 32
Nixon, J. 14
Norman-Jackson, J. 53–4
Nowicki, S. 55–6
Nucci, L. 36, 72–4, 90–3
Nucci, M. S. 73

Odagiri, H. 106
Omelich, C. L. 57
O'Neil, R. P. 88
Osgood, C. E. 62
Osman, L. M. 42

Parke, R. D. 10, 130
Parry, G. 15
Parsons, J. E. 48–51
Parsons, T. 98
Patterson, G. R. 93
Pearlman, B. 3, 133, 136
Peele, S. 17
Pelton, L. H. 13
Perret-Clermont, A. N. 112–13, 115
Perry, D. G. 82
Perry, L. C. 82
Peter, N. 99
Piaget, J. 18, 28, 59, 65, 69–70, 73–4, 76,
    81, 84, 86–7, 90, 112, 114, 119–20
Pike, R. 56
Pilon, D. A. 105
Power, T. G. 10
Prentice, N. M. 90
Prior, J. B. 32
Propper, A. M. 128
Putnam, H. 17

Rablin, J. 62, 65
Radin, N. 130, 132
Radke-Yarrow, M. 65, 69
Renshaw, J. R. 16, 136
Reppucci, N. D. 131
Rest, J. R. 30
Richman, L. C. 93
Robinson, J. 4
Rockwell, R. C. 7
Rodgers, W. L. 11
Rohlen, T. P. 106–7
Rose, D. J. 54
Rosenberg, F. 122

Rosenberg, M. 122
Rosenthal, R. 34
Rosenwald, A. 20
Ross, H. L. 134
Rothbaum, F. 91, 119
Rubenstein, J. L. 74, 80
Rubin, K. H. 19
Ruble, D. N. 48
Russell, G. 41, 132
Russell, J. 32, 113–14
Rutter, M. 30, 96
Ryle, G. 32

Sagi, A. 98
Salili, F. 99
Saltzstein, H. D. 20, 64
Sampson, E. E. 17
Sandler, I. N. 12
Sanford, N. 23
Santrock, J. W. 29, 131
Sasaki, N. 106, 110
Sawhill, I. V. 134
Scarse, R. 100
Schaefer, E. S. 67, 94
Scheck, D. L. 1, 9
Schneider, D. J. 57
Schooler, C. 11
Schwartz, S. 10
Schwarz, J. C. 74
Sears, R. R. 23
Segal, W. 55–6
Selman, R. L. 115–7
Semin, G. R. 57
Shapland, J. 84–5
Shepherd, G. 12
Sherman, D. 12
Shevrin, H. 20
Shore, M. F. 135
Shwalb, D. W. 107, 109
Shweder, R. A. 73, 77, 81
Siegal, M. 35, 41, 56, 61–2, 64–5, 68, 70,
    74, 79, 82, 87, 89, 98, 102–4, 106–9
Simmons, A. G. 122
Simons, R. L. 8
Sinclair, H. 112
Skeen, J. 60
Slater, P. E. 24
Smetana, J. G. 73–6, 78, 105
Smith, D. A. 8
Smith, E. R. 11

Smith, M. B. 122
Smith, N. E. 98
Smithson, M. 99
Snow, M. E. 42
Snyder, S. S. 91, 119
Sohn, D. 48–9
Spenner, K. I. 52
Spivack, G. 122
Staub, E. 134
Stein, A. H. 51
Steinberg, L. D. 14, 74, 134–5
Steinmetz, C. H. D. 94–5
Stoke, S. M. 31
Storey, R. M. 74, 79
Straker, G. 133
Strickland, B. R. 55
Strickland, R. G. 74
Sutherland, E. H. 8

Takezawa, S. 110
Tapp, J. L. 91
Taylor, K. 135
Tesser, A. 105
Thurber, E. 8, 128
Tisak, M. 77, 80
Tittle, C. R. 8
Tribe, V. 98
Trotter, K. T. 19
Tsurumi, Y. 107
Tuma, N. B. 134
Turiel, E. 28, 36, 71–4, 76, 78, 99, 102
Twentyman, C. T. 74, 78
Tygart, C. E. 84

Udolf, R. 87
Underwood, B. 19

Van Dijk, J. J. M. 94–5
Villemez, W. J. 8
Vogel, D. 126

Wagar, J. A. 4
Walker, A. 74
Walker, N. D. 83
Warr, P. 15
Warshak, R. A. 131
Waterman, J. 133
Watson, M. M. 115
Waxler, C. Z. 43
Weiner, B. 46–8, 99

Weiner, I. B. 28, 122
Weis, J. G. 8–9
Weiss, R. 27
Weisz, J. R. 60–1, 91, 119
West, D. J. 9, 126
Weston, D. 71
Wheaton, B. 12
White, K. R. 52
White, P. 33
White, R. W., 26, 33, 54, 56
Whitehill, A. M. 110
Whiteman, M. 86
Wichern, F. 56
Willerman, L. 54
Wilson, H. 93

Wilson, T. D. 33
Winer, B. J. 109
Winocur, S. 103–4, 108
Wolf, D. 134

Yarrow, M. R. 43
Yussen, S. 19

Zahn-Waxler, C. 65, 69
Zajonc, R. B. 20
Zanna, M. P. 85, 87
Zawadski, B. 6
Zeiss, A. 55
Zeiss, R. 55
Zelkowitz, P. 13

Subject Index

ability 5, 11, 45–51, 58, 84, 97, 99, 107–9

achievement 5–6, 16, 45–58, 97–111, 120, 124–5, 132, 137

adolescents 6, 18, 34, 52, 85–91, 98–9, 122–4, 135

affect *see* emotions

attributions
 for achievement 45–58, 99–100, 125
 produced by discipline 59, 69, 82
 for transgressions 86, 120

autonomy 30, 41, 56, 91–3, 105, 119, 121–3, 135

Bayley Scales of Infant Developement 53

Bem Sex Role Inventory 105, 132

birth order 38–40, 42

causality, issues of 10, 15, 35, 43, 58, 83, 133, 138

child abuse 2–3, 11–15, 74, 85, 133

childrearing 6, 10, 15, 59–71, 80–3, 93–6, 105–6, 110, 119–21

Child Report of Parental Behavior Inventory 94

cognitive development 1, 11, 25–42, 53, 101, 103, 115, 120, 125, 130

competence 11, 26, 55

conflict
 between cognitions 20, 28, 112–14
 between parents 7, 9–10, 126, 131
 between work and family 16, 97, 136
 in parent-child relations 112, 121–4, 131, 134
 in peer relations 73, 81, 113–4

conscience *see* guilt

control
 locus of 55–6
 primary and secondary 91, 119–24
 see also childrearing, parents

daycare 73–81, 136

delinquency 2–3, 5–11, 15, 83–4, 89–96, 135

distributive justice 28, 101–2, 114

divorce 131

drugs 9, 13, 83, 86

economic deprivation 2–15, 84–8, 98–103, 132–6

education 4, 8, 10–11, 42, 47, 54, 71, 75

effort *see* ability

egocentrism 32, 59–61, 70, 76, 78, 80–82, 91, 101, 112–13, 115, 125

emotions 20, 23, 26, 28, 31, 43, 47, 55, 64–5, 69, 72, 81, 83, 110, 116–18, 125–6

empathy 30, 41, 103

equality 3–4, 100–1, 107

equity 77, 100
 see also distributive justice

exosystem 4–5, 16–17, 97, 102–3

fairness 41, 100–3

family 2–17, 20, 52, 88, 93, 97–8, 106–10, 126–38

fathers 7, 9–11, 21, 26, 35–42, 49–50, 56, 60, 70, 75, 97–8, 105, 110, 115, 127–32, 134

friendship *see* peers

General Health Questionnaire 12

guilt 21, 33–4, 48, 64, 120–1

helping 59, 77, 79–80

heredity 13, 54

identification 20–44, 81–2, 104

imitation and modelling 23–6, 59

immanent justice 120–2

induction and reasoning as discipline 59, 64–9

Intellectual Responsibility Achievement Scale 55
intelligence *see* achievement, cognitive development
intentionality 60, 77, 84, 87, 91
internalization 21, 23, 25, 35, 42, 51, 82

law 9, 16, 18, 84–91, 122
love withdrawal as discipline 26, 64–9

macrosystem 16–17
maternal employment 51, 127–9
mathematics 49–51, 56, 58
mental health 11–13, 15, 84–5, 132
mesosystem 4, 16–17, 51, 97, 102–3
microsystem 4–5, 15, 17, 51, 97, 102–3, 138
moral development, 16, 18–44, 71–82, 90, 120–5

Nowicki–Strickland Locus of Control Scales 55

Oedipus complex 21, 23–4, 31

parents
    expectations of 45, 49–58, 137
    and parenthood 1, 16, 58, 126, 137
Peabody Picture Vocabulary Test 54
peers 36, 38, 40, 52, 73–82, 92, 94–6, 125
permissiveness 60–9, 93–6, 125
power as discipline 21, 64–9, 105, 110, 121–4, 127
psychoanalytic theory 21–4, 31, 64, 82, 120–2
punishment 18, 23, 59, 64–5, 69, 76, 82–3, 85–6, 92, 115–17, 120

reading 37–40, 53–4, 56
role-taking 19, 25–8
    see also egocentrism

school *see* education
self-definition 20, 32, 41–3, 103, 105, 118–9, 125
self-efficacy 11, 54, 56
self-knowledge 32
sex differences 6–7, 16, 26–7, 37, 42, 46–7, 51, 63
sex roles 24, 26–7, 30, 32, 35, 40–3, 103, 132
siblings 61
social class differences 3, 8, 13–14, 19, 34, 46, 63, 99, 102, 132
social cognition 35, 40, 74–6, 82
social conventions 71–82, 91–2, 96, 103
social learning 23, 25, 82, 125
society and culture
    American 3, 84
    Australian 4, 85, 106–7
    British 4, 100
    Danish 9
    English 84–5
    Japanese 98, 106–11
    Swedish 100
    Western industrial 2, 5, 51, 97–9, 136
symbolic interactionism 1, 23, 119

television 54, 92, 126

unemployment 10–14, 132, 136

welfare policy
    bubble-up 3–4, 126–38
    trickle-down 2–15, 85, 133–8
withdrawal of love *see* love withdrawal as discipline